About Phonics Connection:

Welcome to RBP Books' Connection series. Like our Summer Bridge Activities collection, this series is designed to make learning fun and rewarding. Connection Phonics books are based on the premise that mastering language skills builds confidence and enhances a student's entire educational experience. A fundamental factor in learning to read is a strong phonics foundation, beginning with an awareness of the alphabet, understanding phonemic relationships and the concept of words, and moving onto word recognition. This workbook is based on core curriculum and is designed to reinforce classroom phonics skills and strategies. Pages include graphics, examples, and simple directions to introduce phonics concepts such as letter and sound recognition, word families, long and short vowels, blends, sight words, beginning and ending sounds, contractions, plurals, prefixes and suffixes, antonyms and synonyms, homophones, and silent letters. Phonics Connection books also provide writing practice.

Dear Parents and Educators,

Thank you for choosing this Rainbow Bridge Publishing educational product to help teach your children and students. We take great pride and pleasure in becoming involved with your educational experience. Some people say that math will always be math and reading will always be reading, but we do not share that opinion. Reading, math, spelling, writing, geography, science, history, and all other subjects will always be some of life's most fulfilling adventures and should be taught with passion both at home and in the classroom. Because of this, we at Rainbow Bridge Publishing associate the greatness of learning with every product we create.

It is our mission to provide materials that not only explain, but also amaze; not only review, but also encourage; not only guide, but also lead. Every product contains clear, concise instructions, appropriate sample work, and engaging, grade-appropriate content created by classroom teachers and writers that is based on national standards to support your best educational efforts. We hope you enjoy our company's products as you embark on your adventure. Thank you for bringing us along.

Sincerely,

George Starks
Associate Publisher
Rainbow Bridge Publishing

Phonics Connection™ • Grade 1
Written by Clareen Nelson-Arnold

For information, call or write: Rainbow Bridge Publishing, Inc. • PO Box 571470 • Salt Lake City, Utah 84157-1470 • Tel: (801) 268-8887

Illustrations
Amanda Sorensen

Visual Design and Layout
Andy Carlson, Robyn Funk, Zachary Johnson, Scott Whimpey

Publisher
Scott G. Van Leeuwen

Associate Publisher
George Starks

Series Creator
Michele Van Leeuwen

Editorial Director
Paul Rawlins

Copy Editors and Proofreaders
Aimee Hansen, Elaine Clark

Technology Integration
James Morris, Dante J. Orazzi

Please visit our website at
www.summerbridgeactivities.com
for supplements, additions, and corrections to this book.

First Edition 2003

For orders call 1-800-598-1441
Discounts available for quantity orders

ISBN: 1-932210-23-7

PRINTED IN THE UNITED STATES OF AMERICA
10 9 8 7 6 5 4 3 2 1

Phonics - Grade 1
Table of Contents

Sound and Letters Chart

rat ă	ape ā	snail ai	crayfish ā
bear b	cat c	centipede s	cheetah ch
deer d	elephant ě	seal ē	bee ē
fish f	gorilla g	giraffe j	horse h
inchworm ĭ	crocodile ī	jaguar j	kangaroo k
lion l	mouse m	newt n	gong ng

www.summerbridgeactivities.com Phonics Connection—Grade 1—RBP0237

Sound and Letters Chart

dŏg ŏ	gōat ō	stōne ō	gōōse ōō
wōōd ōō	crōw ow	pig p	quail qu
rabbit r	skunk s	shark sh	turtle t
thrust th	dŭck ŭ	Dūke ū	vulture v
wolf w	whale wh	Fox x	xylophone x
yak y	fly y	pony y	zebra z

Phonics Connection—Grade 1—RBP0237   www.summerbridgeactivities.com   © RBP Books

Bb Mm Hh

Say each picture name. Listen to the **first sound**. Print the upper- and lowercase letter that stands for the first sound.

Review of consonant sounds *b, m,* and *h* in initial position.

www.summerbridgeactivities.com **Phonics Connection—Grade 1—RBP0237**

Bb Mm

Say each picture name. Listen to the **last sound**. Print the upper- and lowercase letter that stands for the last sound.

M m

Review of consonant sounds for *b* and *m* in final position.

www.summerbridgeactivities.com

© RBP Books

Pp Ww Tt

Say each picture name. Listen to the **first sound**. Print the upper- and lowercase letter that stands for the first sound.

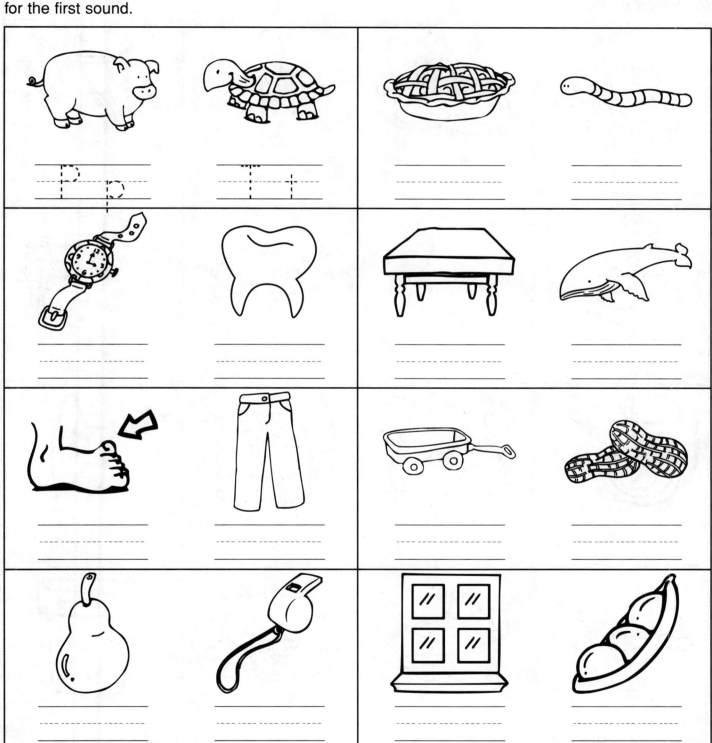

Review of consonant sounds for *p, w,* and *t* in initial position.

www.summerbridgeactivities.com   **Phonics Connection—Grade 1—RBP0237**

Pp Tt

Say each picture name. Listen to the **last sound**. Print the upper- and lowercase letter that stands for the last sound.

Review of consonant sounds for *p* and *t* in final position.

Jj Nn Kk

Say each picture name. Listen to the **first sound**. Print the upper- and lowercase letter that stands for the first sound.

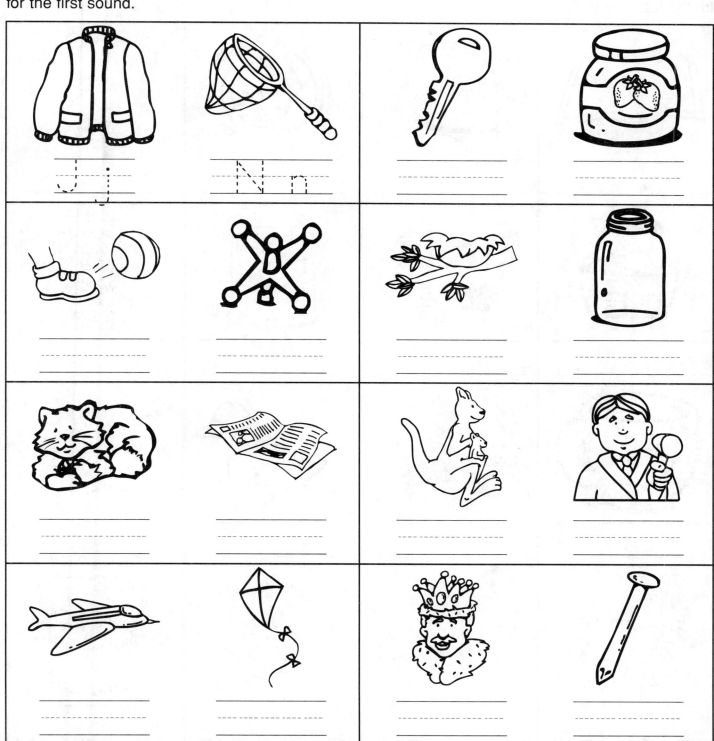

J j   N n   _____   _____

_____   _____   _____   _____

_____   _____   _____   _____

_____   _____   _____   _____

Review of consonant sounds for *j*, *n*, and *k* in initial position.

Nn Kk

Say each picture name. Listen to the **last sound**. Print the upper- and lowercase letter that stands for the last sound.

Review of consonant sounds for *n* and *k* in final position.

Phonics Connection—Grade 1—RBP0237
www.summerbridgeactivities.com
©RBP Books

Ff Ll Yy

Say each picture name. Listen to the **first sound**. Print the upper- and lowercase letter that stands for the first sound.

Review of consonant sounds for *f*, *y*, and *l* in initial position.

www.summerbridgeactivities.com   **Phonics Connection—Grade 1—RBP0237**

Name

Ff Ll

Say each picture name. Listen to the **last sound**. Print the upper- and lowercase letter that stands for the last sound.

Review of consonant sounds for *f* or *l* in final position.

Phonics Connection—Grade 1—RBP0237

14

www.summerbridgeactivities.com

© RBP Books

Name

Rr Ss Vv

Say each picture name. Listen to the **first sound**. Print the upper- and lowercase letter that stands for the first sound.

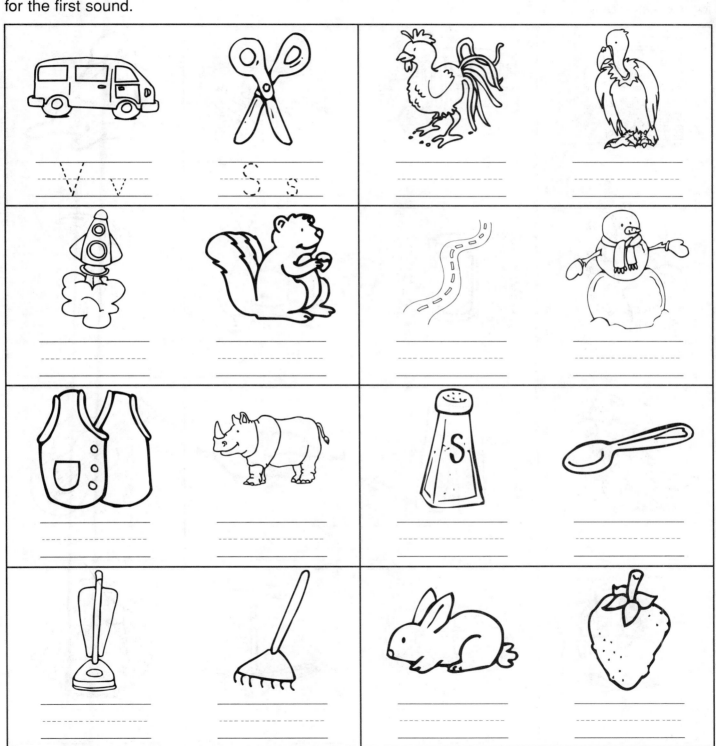

Review of consonant sounds for *v*, *r*, and *s* in initial position.

© RBP Books   www.summerbridgeactivities.com   Phonics Connection—Grade 1—RBP0237

Name

Rr Ss

Say each picture name. Listen to the **last sound**. Print the upper- and lowercase letter that stands for the last sound.

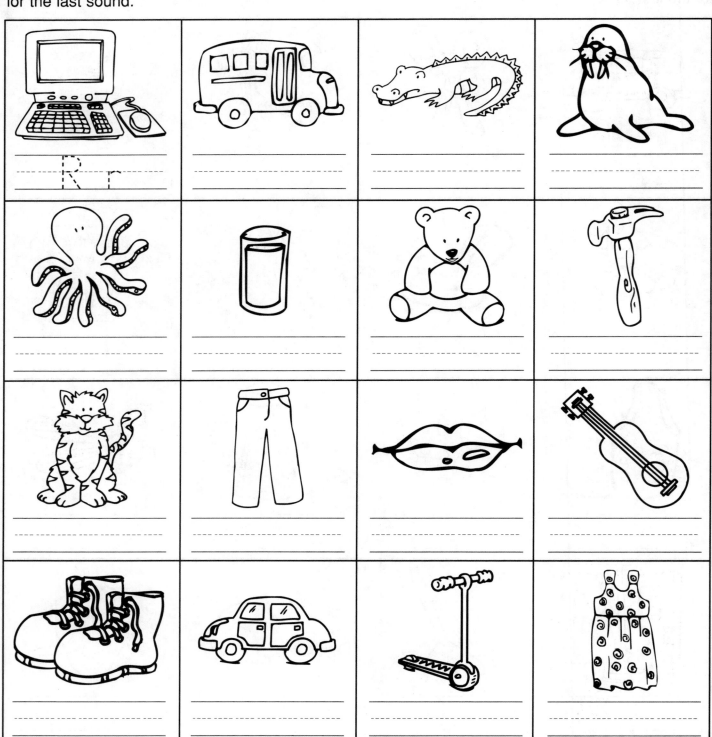

Review of consonant sounds for *r* and *s* in final position.

www.summerbridgeactivities.com

Dd Qq Xx

Say each picture name. Listen to the **first sound**. Print the upper- and lowercase letter that stands for the first sound.

Review of consonant sounds for *d*, *q*, and *x* in initial position.

www.summerbridgeactivities.com   **Phonics Connection—Grade 1—RBP0237**

Name

Dd Xx

Say each picture name. Listen to the **last sound**. Print the upper- and lowercase letter that stands for the last sound.

Review of consonant sounds for *d* and *x* in final position.

Cc Gg Zz

Say each picture name. Listen to the **first sound**. Print the upper- and lowercase letter that stands for the first sound.

Review of consonant sounds for c, g, and z in initial position.

www.summerbridgeactivities.com Phonics Connection—Grade 1—RBP0237

Cc Gg Zz

Say each picture name. Listen to the **last sound**. Print the upper- and lowercase letter that stands for the last sound.

Review of consonant sounds for *c*, *g*, and *z* in final position.

Name

Consonants

Say the name of the picture. Listen to the **first sound**. Fill in the bubble next to the letter that stands for the first sound you hear. Write the letter.

www.summerbridgeactivities.com **Phonics Connection—Grade 1—RBP0237**

Name

Consonants

Say the name of the picture. Listen to the **final sound**. Fill in the bubble next to the letter that stands for the final sound you hear. Write the letter.

Phonics Connection—Grade 1—RBP0237   www.summerbridgeactivities.com   ©RBP Books

Name

Aa

Say each picture name. Listen for the **short *a*** sound \ă\ as in *apple*. Color the picture if its name has the short *a* sound.

Introducing the short *a* sound \ă\.

www.summerbridgeactivities.com Phonics Connection—Grade 1—RBP0237

Aa

Look at the letters in the rubber band. Stretch out the sounds; then snap them together to make the word. Say "b—" "a—" "t—" "bat." Print the word.

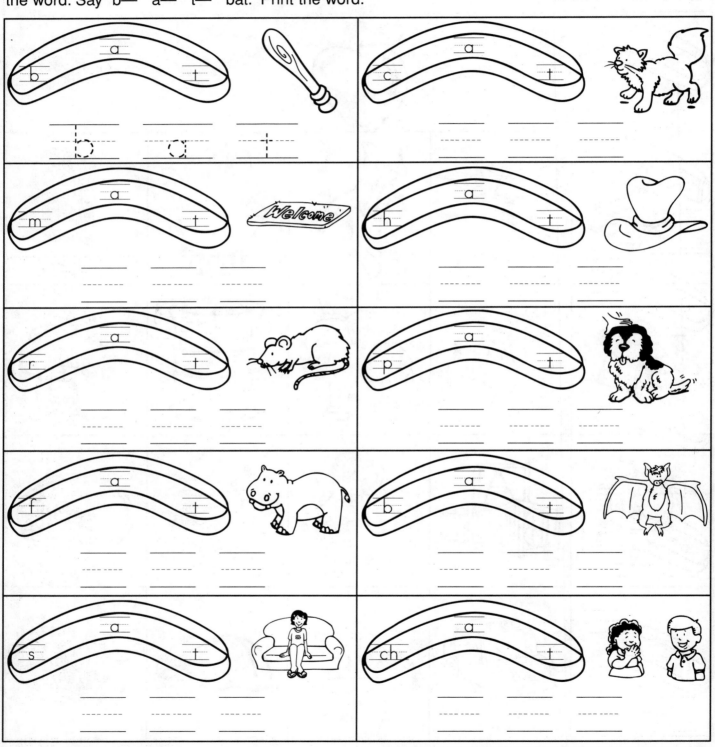

b a t

b a t

c a t

m a t

h a t

r a t

p a t

f a t

b a t

s a t

ch a t

Using the sound of short *a*; word chunk *at*.

Phonics Connection—Grade 1—RBP0237

www.summerbridgeactivities.com

Name _____

Aa

Look at the letters in the rubber band. Stretch out the sounds; then snap them together to make the word. Say "c—" "a—" "n—" "can." Print the word. Draw a line from the word to the picture.

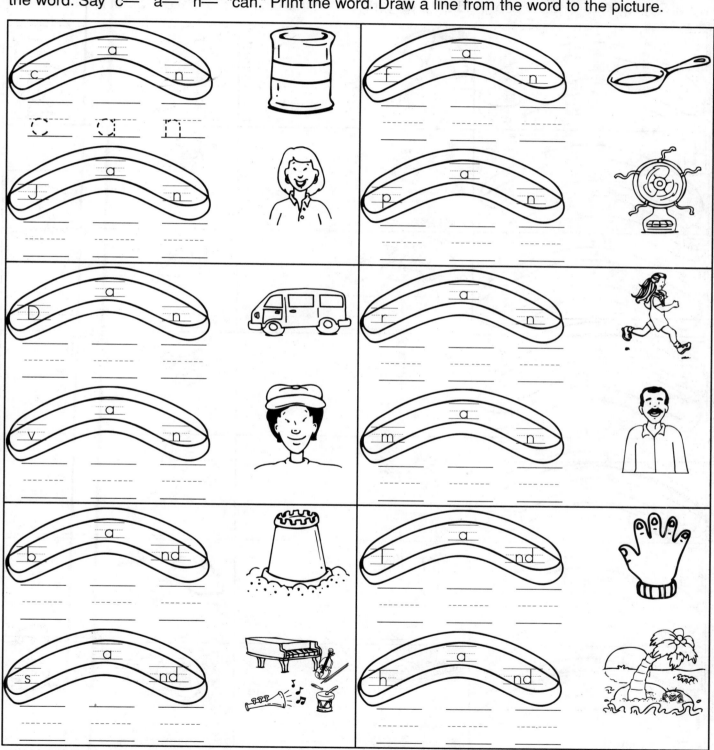

Using the sound of short *a*; word chunks *an* and *and*.

www.summerbridgeactivities.com

Phonics Connection—Grade 1—RBP0237

Aa

Look at the letters in the rubber band. Stretch out the sounds; then snap them together to make the word. Say "c—" "a—" "p—" "cap." Add the beginning sound from the box to make a word. Print the word.

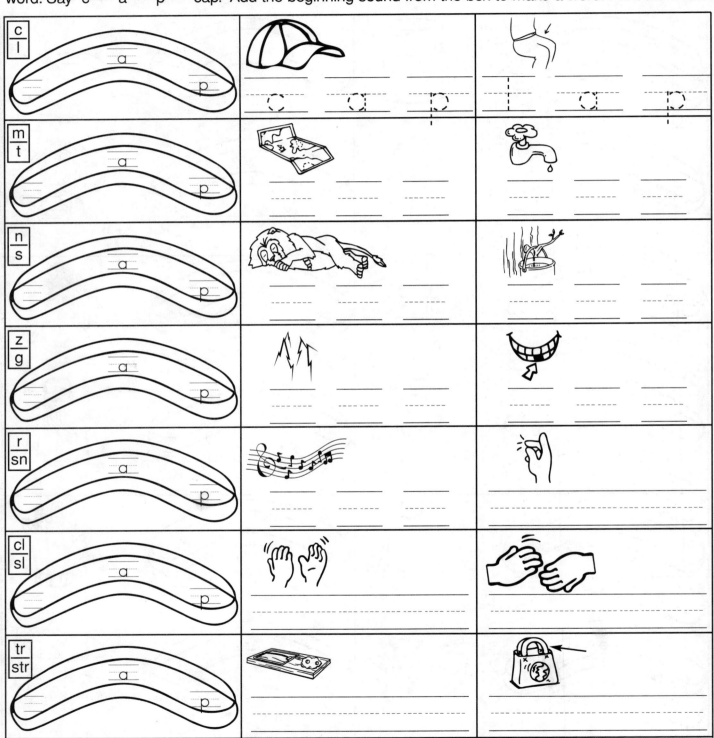

Using the sound of short *a*; word chunk *ap*.

Name

Aa

Look at the letters in the rubber band. Stretch out the sounds; then snap them together to make the word. Say "c—" "a—" "n—" "can." Add the ending chunk from the box to make a word. Print the word.

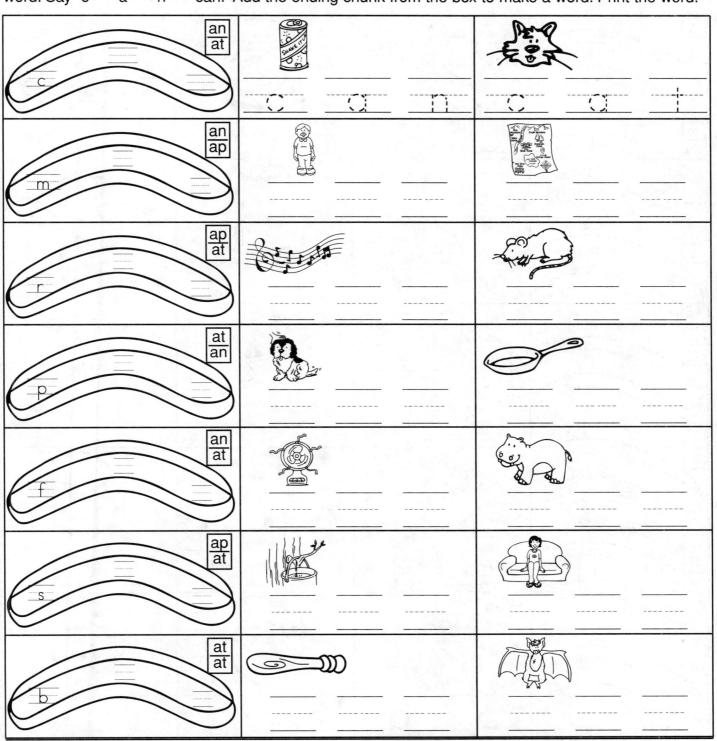

Using the sound of short *a*; word chunks *at*, *an*, and, *ap*; final sounds.

www.summerbridgeactivities.com   Phonics Connection—Grade 1—RBP0237

Name

Aa

Say each picture name. Listen for the **short a** sound \ă\. Print a if you hear the short a sound.

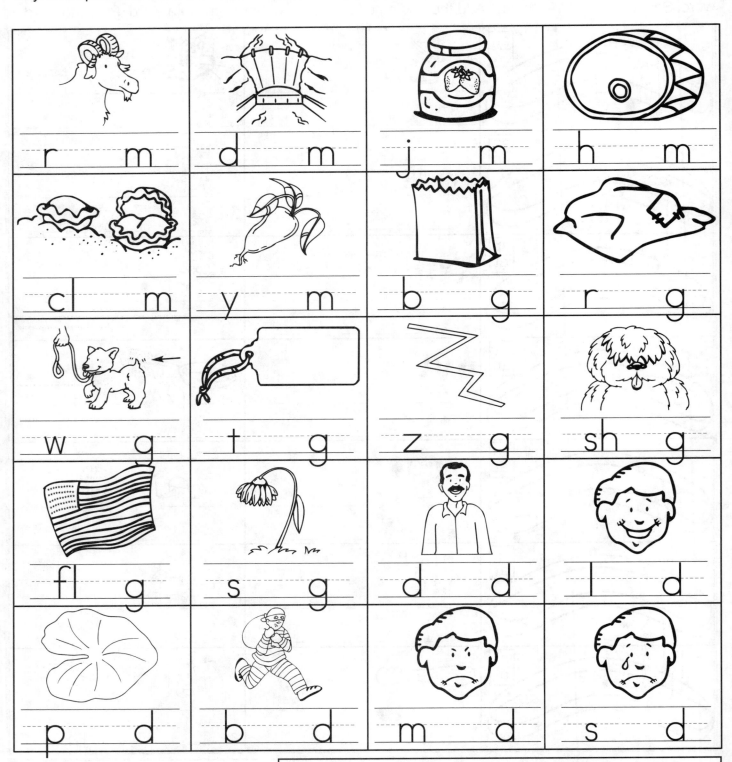

r ___ m	d ___ m	j ___ m	h ___ m
c ___ m	y ___ m	b ___ g	r ___ g
w ___ g	t ___ g	z ___ g	sh ___ g
f ___ g	s ___ g	d ___ d	l ___ d
p ___ d	b ___ d	m ___ d	s ___ d

Using the sound of short a; review of the middle short a word chunks am, ag, ad.

www.summerbridgeactivities.com

Name

Aa

Say each picture name. Listen to the sounds. Print the word.

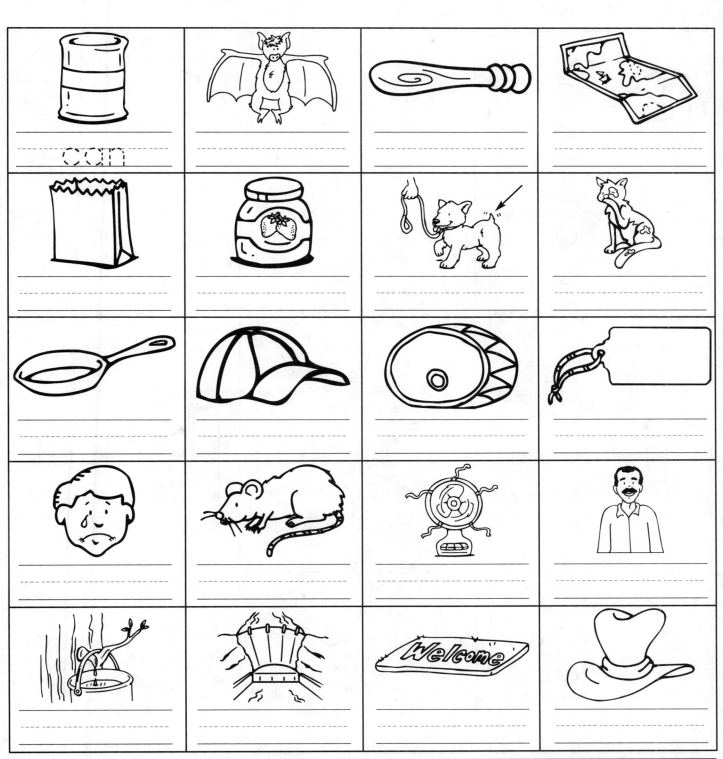

can

Using the sound of short *a*; review short *a* word chunks *at*, *an*, *ad*, *ag*, *ab*, *am*, *and*, *ap*, and *as*.

www.summerbridgeactivities.com   Phonics Connection—Grade 1—RBP0237

Name

Aa

Say each picture name. Listen to each sound. Fill in the bubble next to the word made by the sounds. Print the word for the picture.

○ cat	
○ can	
● cap	

cap

| ○ fat |
| ○ fan |
| ○ fad |

| ○ sat |
| ○ sad |
| ○ sap |

| ○ mat |
| ○ man |
| ○ mad |

| ○ bat |
| ○ bad |
| ○ bag |

| ○ rat |
| ○ rag |
| ○ ran |

| ○ pat |
| ○ pan |
| ○ pam |

| ○ hat |
| ○ hand |
| ○ ham |

| ○ nat |
| ○ nap |
| ○ nag |

| ○ cat |
| ○ bat |
| ○ rat |

| ○ map |
| ○ lap |
| ○ tap |

| ○ ram |
| ○ dam |
| ○ jam |

Using the sound of short *a*; word chunks; standardized testing form.

Phonics Connection—Grade 1—RBP0237   www.summerbridgeactivities.com   ©RBP Books

Name _____

Aa

Game with **short a** words. Begin the game at the word *Start*. Toss a die to determine how many squares you can move. Say the word you land on. If you can not say the word, go back one space. The one who lands on *Finish* first wins.

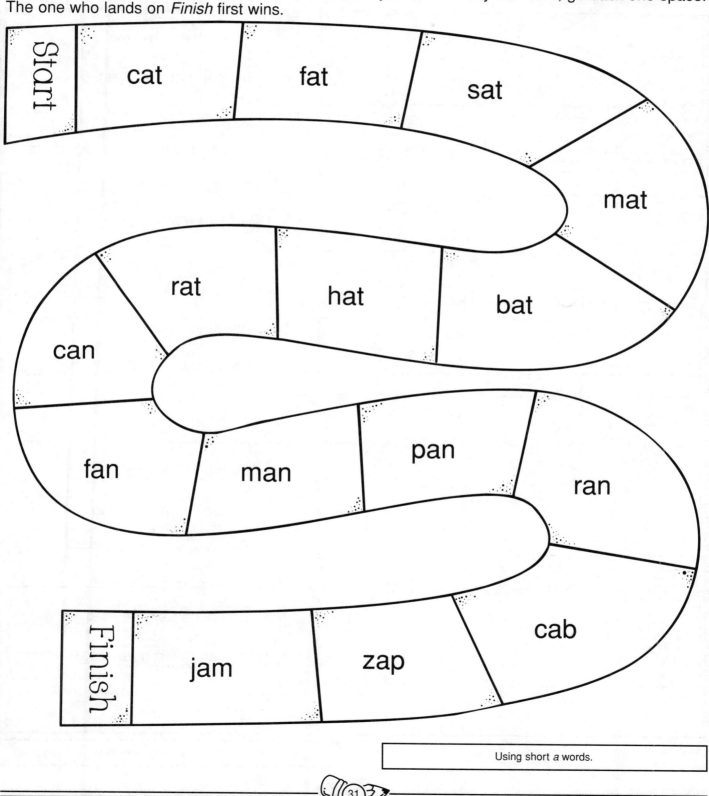

Start

cat

fat

sat

mat

rat

hat

bat

can

fan

man

pan

ran

cab

Finish

jam

zap

Using short *a* words.

© RBP Books   www.summerbridgeactivities.com   Phonics Connection—Grade 1—RBP0237

Name

Aa

Read each sentence. Listen to each sound. Fill in one bubble. Print that sentence. Draw a picture of that sentence.

	● The cat has a red hat. ○ The man has a red hat.

The cat has a red hat.

	○ Dad had a blue van. ○ Dad had a blue can.

	○ The rat sat on the yellow mat. ○ The rat sat on the yellow bat.

	○ The brown cat can wag. ○ The brown bat can wag.

	○ The fan had a green tag. ○ The can had a green tag.

Recognizing short *a* words.

Phonics Connection—Grade 1—RBP0237   www.summerbridgeactivities.com   ©RBP Books

Aa

Read each sentence. Print a word that rhymes with the underlined word. Make the sentence tell about the picture to the right.

1. The fat <u>cat</u> sat on a bat_____.

2. The man had a <u>tag</u> on a _____.

3. Pam is <u>sad</u> and _____.

4. <u>Max</u> had an _____.

5. Jan has a <u>pan</u> and a _____.

6. The <u>cap</u> is on the _____.

7. Dad had a <u>nap</u> on the _____.

8. Sam had <u>jam</u> and _____.

Using language arts; rhyming words; using context clues to select rhyming words with short *a* chunks.

Aa

Read each sentence. Read the three words. Look at the picture. Fill in the bubble next to the word that makes sense in the sentence. Print the word on the line.

1. Dan has a **bat**.	● bat ○ wag ○ had	
2. Max had a _____.	○ ram ○ pat ○ sad	
3. Dad has a _____.	○ land ○ sand ○ band	
4. Ann sat on a _____.	○ cab ○ hat ○ bad	
5. The rat ran to the _____.	○ wax ○ rap ○ lad	
6. Zack had a _____.	○ ham ○ sand ○ fad	

Using language arts; using context clues to select missing words with short *a* chunks.

Aa

Read the words. Look at the picture. Write the words in the correct order to match the picture.

The	the
cat	on
is	rat

The rat is on the cat.

bat	the
is	in
The	can

ram	the
fan	on
The	is

the	ham
pan	in
is	The

Using language arts; using context clues to write sentences; using short *a* word chunks.

www.summerbridgeactivities.com   **Phonics Connection—Grade 1—RBP0237**

Name

Aa

Write the name of the picture. Read the sentences below, and color each picture. Underline the **short a** words in the sentence.

rat

The rat is yellow.   The can is blue.   The cap is red.   The ham is blue.

The bag is red.   The dad is yellow.   The bat is blue.   The fan is red.

Language arts application; short *a* word chunks.

Name

Aa

Read the story below. Say each word. Listen carefully for the **short _a_** sound \ă\. Draw a line under each word with the short _a_ sound. Draw pictures of what is happening in the story as you read it.

<u>Pam</u> is a <u>bat</u>.

She is a fat bat.

She landed on a hat.

She landed on Dad's hat.

Dad was mad.

Dad was sad.

His hat looked bad.

Read the story once more. Read the questions below. Fill in the bubble by the correct answer.

1. Is Pam a bat?   no ◯ yes ◯

2. Is Pam a fat bat?   no ◯ yes ◯

3. Did Pam sit on the map?   no ◯ yes ◯

4. Did Dad get mad at Pam?   no ◯ yes ◯

Write a title for the story. _____

Tell a friend what might happen next in the story.

> Language arts application; reading and answering comprehension questions with short _a_ word chunks.

 ©RBP Books   www.summerbridgeactivities.com   **Phonics Connection—Grade 1—RBP0237**

Name _____

Ii

Say each picture name. Listen for the **short *i*** sound \ĭ\ as in *fish*. Color the picture if its name has the short *i* sound.

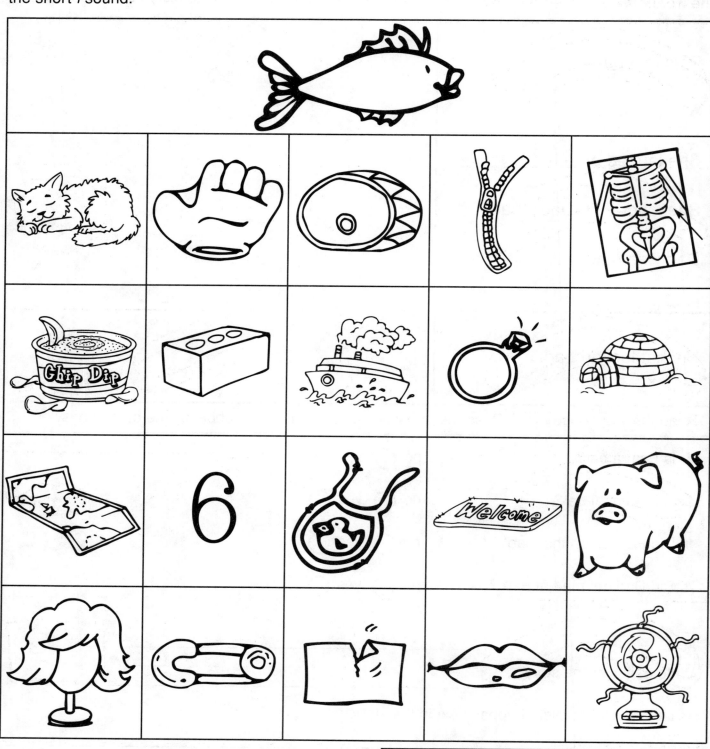

Introducing the short *i* sound \ĭ\.

Phonics Connection—Grade 1—RBP0237

38

www.summerbridgeactivities.com

© **RBP Books**

Name

Ii

Look at the letters in the rubber band. Stretch out the sounds; then snap them together to make the word. Say "s—" "i—" "t—" "sit." Print the word.

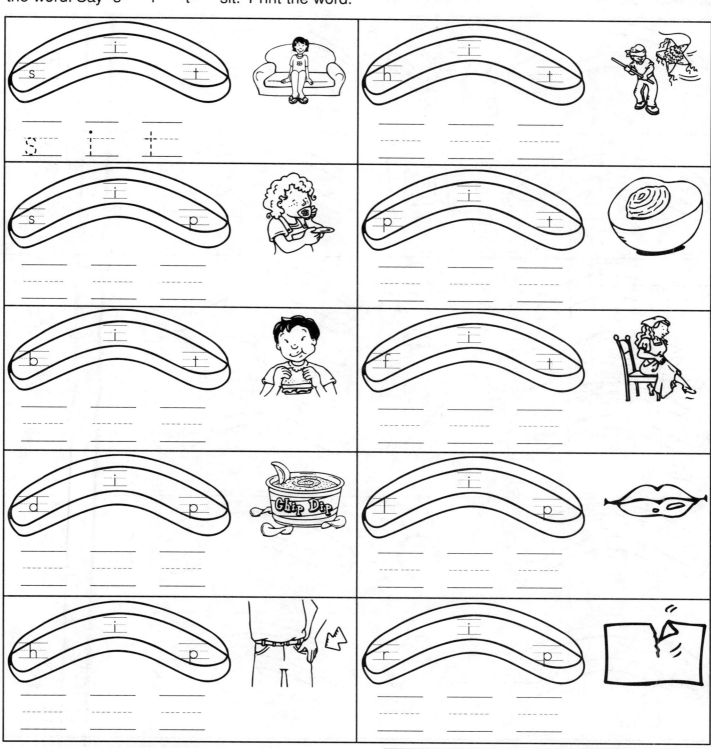

s   i   t

s i t

s   i   p

b   i   t

d   i   p

h   i   p

h   i   t

p   i   t

f   i   t

l   i   p

r   i   p

Using the sound of short *i*; word chunks *it* and *ip*.

www.summerbridgeactivities.com   **Phonics Connection—Grade 1—RBP0237**

Ii

Look at the letters in the rubber band. Stretch out the sounds; then snap them together to make the word. Say "f—" "i—" "n—" "fin." Print the word. Draw a line from the word to the picture.

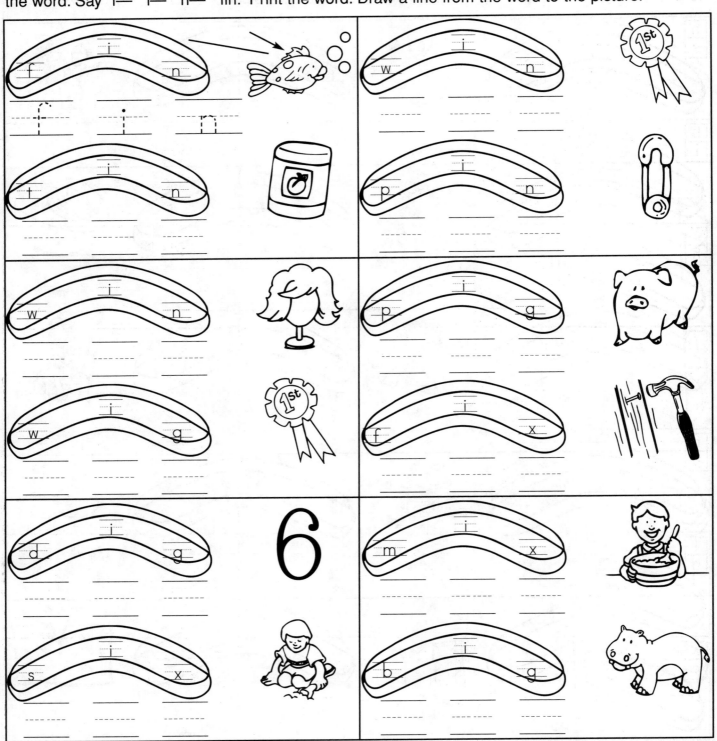

Using the sound of short *i*; word chunks *in*, *ig*, and *ix*.

Phonics Connection—Grade 1—RBP0237   www.summerbridgeactivities.com   ©RBP Books

Ii

Look at the letters in the rubber band. Stretch out the sounds; then snap them together to make the word. Say "h—" "i—" "t—" "hit." Add the beginning sound from the box to make a word. Print the word.

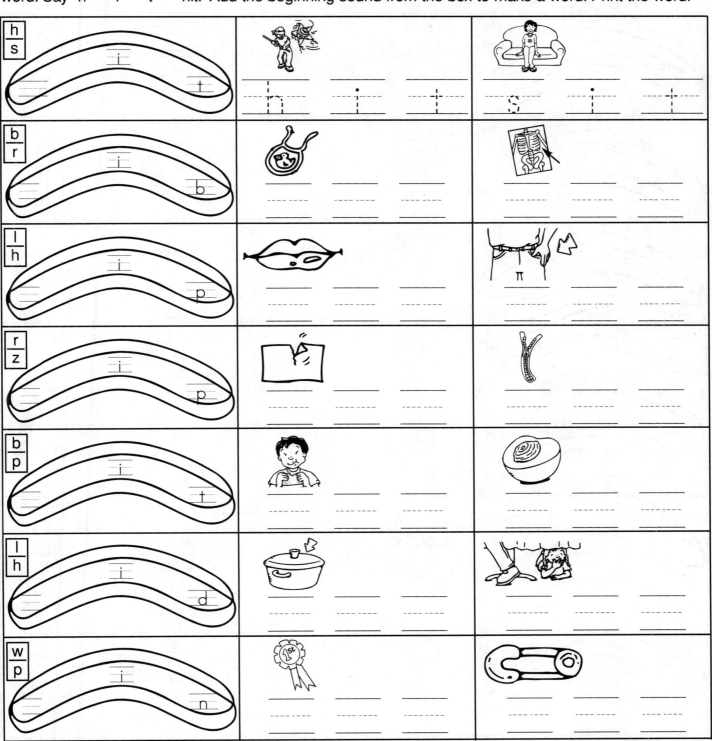

Using the sound of short *i*; word chunks *it*, *ip*, *in*, *id*, and *ib*.

www.summerbridgeactivities.com Phonics Connection—Grade 1—RBP0237

Ii

Look at the letters in the rubber band. Stretch out the sounds; then snap them together to make the word. Say "p—" "i—" "g—" "pig." Add the ending chunk from the box to make a word. Print the word.

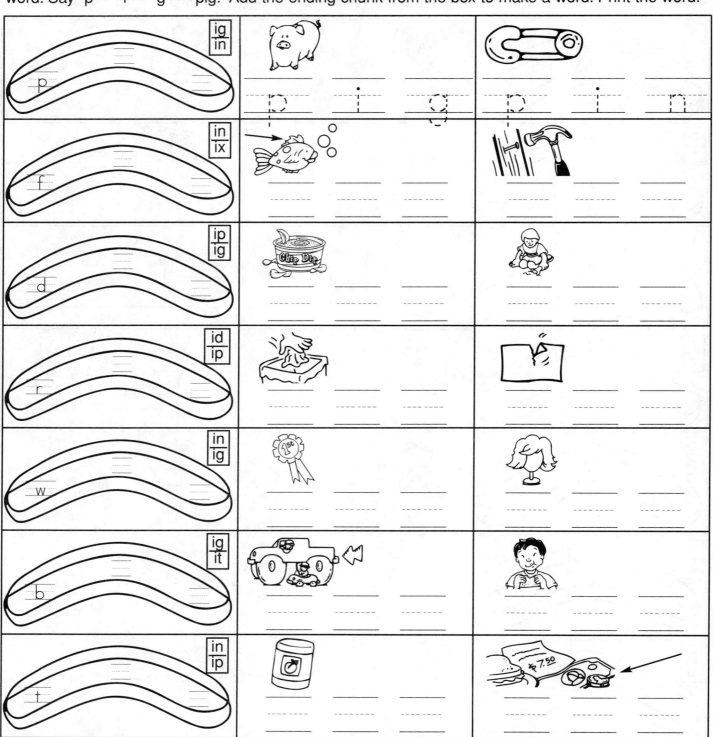

Name

Ii

Say each picture name. Listen for the **short *i*** sound \ĭ\. Print the *i* where you hear the short *i* sound.

f __ t	b __ t	h __ t	p __ t
s __ t	h __ d	l __ d	w __ n
t __ n	p __ n	f __ n	d __ p
p __ g	f __ x	m __ x	s __ x
r __ b	b __ b	p __ ll	h __ ll

Using the sound of short *i*; word chunks *it, ip, in, ig, ix, id, ib,* and *ill*.

43

Name

Ii

Say each picture name. Listen to the sounds. Print the word.

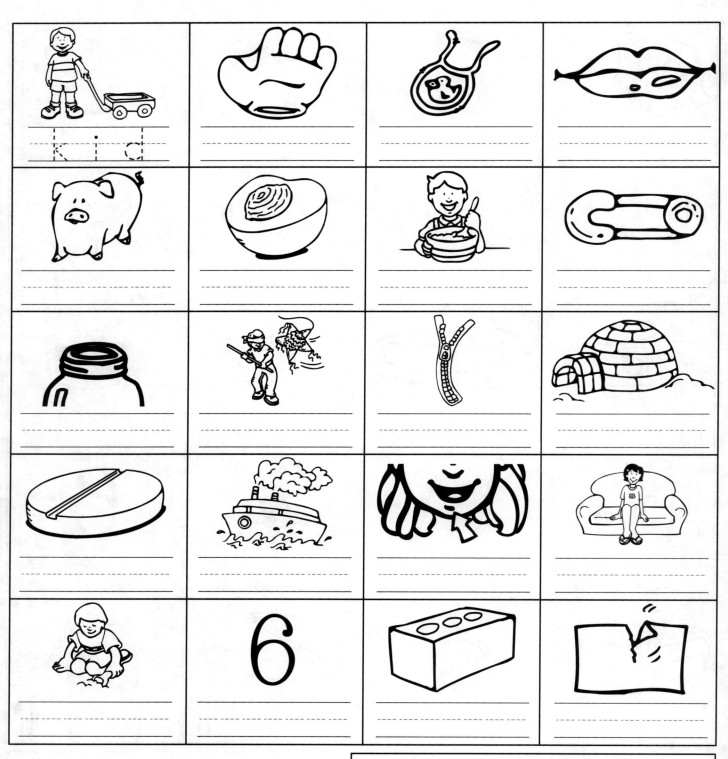

Using the sound of short *i*; word chunks *it, ip, in, ig, ix,* and *ill*.

44

Name

Ii

Say each picture name. Listen to each sound. Fill in the bubble for the picture word, and then print the word.

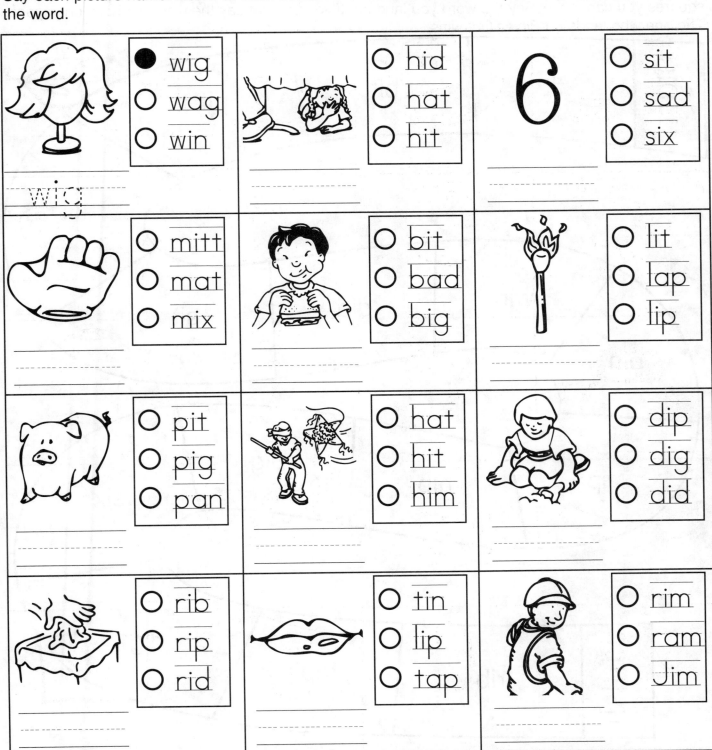

● wig	○ hid
○ wag	○ hat
○ win	○ hit

wig

○ sit	
○ sad	
○ six	

○ mitt	○ bit
○ mat	○ bad
○ mix	○ big

○ lit
○ tap
○ lip

○ pit	○ hat
○ pig	○ hit
○ pan	○ him

○ dip
○ dig
○ did

○ rib	○ tin
○ rip	○ lip
○ rid	○ tap

○ rim
○ ram
○ Jim

Using the sound of short *i*; standardized testing form.

www.summerbridgeactivities.com

Phonics Connection—Grade 1—RBP0237

Name

Ii

Game with **short *i*** words. Begin the game at the word *Start*. Toss a dice to determine how many squares you can move. Say the word you land on. If you can not say the word, go back one space. The one who lands on *Finish* first wins.

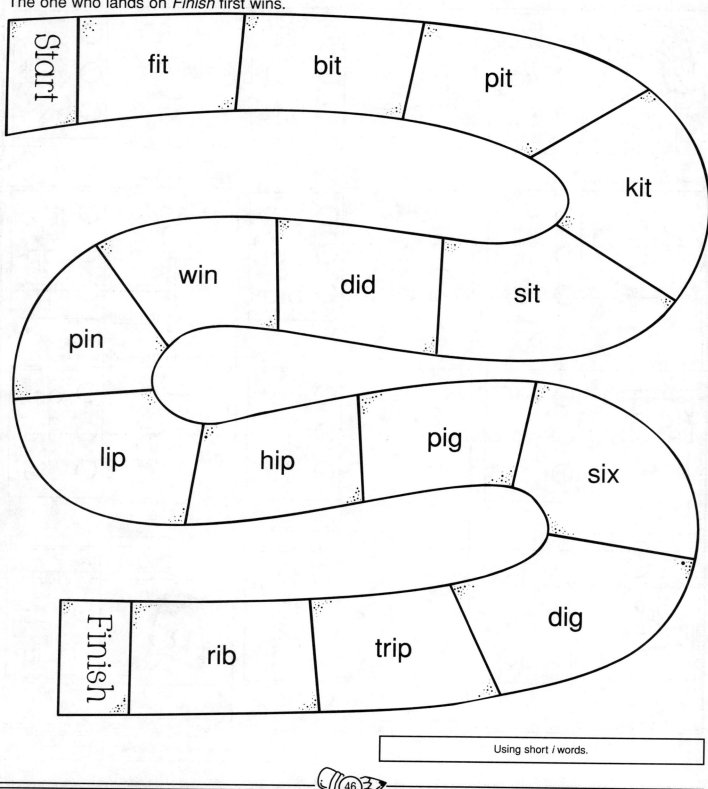

Start

fit

bit

pit

kit

win

did

sit

pin

lip

hip

pig

six

Finish

rib

trip

dig

Using short *i* words.

Phonics Connection—Grade 1—RBP0237

www.summerbridgeactivities.com

©RBP Books

Ii

Read each sentence. Listen to each sound. Fill in one bubble. Print that sentence. Draw a picture of that sentence

● Kit has six red wigs.

○ Kit has six red kits.

Kit has six red wigs.

○ Sid had a blue lip.

○ Sid had a blue hip.

○ The kid sat on the yellow mitt.

○ The kid sat on the yellow mix.

○ The brown pig can dig in a pit.

○ The brown pig can sit on a wig.

○ Liz had a big green ring.

○ Liz had a big green fish.

Recognizing short *i* words.

Name

Ii

Read each sentence. Print a word that rhymes with the underlined word. Make the sentence tell about the picture to the right.

1. The igloo will not <u>fit</u> in the mitt _____.

2. Tim <u>hid</u> the _____.

3. Jim <u>will</u> go up the _____.

4. The <u>fish</u> is in the _____.

5. You take a <u>pill</u> when you are _____.

6. Kim the <u>pig</u> can do a _____.

7. Rob can <u>fix</u> a _____.

8. The <u>wig</u> is too _____.

Using language arts; using context clues to select rhyming words with short *i* word chunks.

Phonics Connection—Grade 1—RBP0237   www.summerbridgeactivities.com   ©**RBP Books**

Name _____

Ii

Read each sentence. Read the three words. Look at the picture. Fill in the bubble next to the word that makes sense in the sentence. Print the word on the line.

1. Kim has a _wig_ .	○ bit ● wig ○ hid	
2. Jim had a _____ .	○ pig ○ pit ○ sid	
3. Kit can _____ a ball.	○ ring ○ sang ○ hit	
4. Liz sat on a _____ .	○ pin ○ hit ○ lip	
5. The fish was on the _____ .	○ dish ○ dig ○ dip	
6. Sid had _____ bells.	○ six ○ sand ○ zip	

Using language arts; using context clues to select missing words with the short *i* sound.

©RBP Books   www.summerbridgeactivities.com   Phonics Connection—Grade 1—RBP0237

Ii

Look at the picture. Write the words in the correct order to match the picture.

The	the
bib	on
is	kid

The bib is on the kid.

fish	the
is	on
The	wig

_____

- - - - - - - - - - - - - - - - .

kit	the
pig	on
The	is

_____

- - - - - - - - - - - - - - - - .

the	igloo
pin	on
is	The

_____

- - - - - - - - - - - - - - - - .

Using language arts; using context clues to write sentences; using short *i* word chunks.

Ii

Write the name of the picture. Read the sentences below and color each picture. Underline the **short *i*** words in each sentence.

pig

The pig is yellow.   The pin is blue.   The wig is red.   The hill is blue.

The mitt is red.   The fin is yellow.   The lip is blue.   The mix is red.

Language arts application; short *i* word chunks *it*, *ip*, *in*, *ig*, *ix*, and *ill*.

www.summerbridgeactivities.com   **Phonics Connection—Grade 1—RBP0237**

Ii

Read the story below. Say each word. Listen carefully for the **short *i*** sound \ĭ\. Draw a line under each word with the short *i* sound. Draw pictures of what is happening in the story as you read it.

This <u>is</u> a <u>big</u> <u>wig</u>.
Who will it fit?

This is Kim.
Kim is a big pig.

Kim the big pig has a wig.
Will it fit a big pig?

No, no, no!

Six thin rats have the wig.
Will six thin rats fit in the wig?

No, no, no!

Sixty hip chicks have the wig.
Will it fit the hip chicks?

No, no, no!

Then, who?
You!
Will you fit in the wig?

Read the story once more. Read the questions below. Fill in the bubble by the correct answer.

1. Is Sid a pig?   no ◯   yes ◯

2. Did the rats fit in the wig?   no ◯   yes ◯

3. Did the chicks fit the wig?   no ◯   yes ◯

4. Did you fit in the wig?   no ◯   yes ◯

Write a title for the story. _____

_____

Tell a friend what might happen next in the story.

Language arts application; reading and answering comprehension questions with short *i* word chunks.

Uu

Say each picture name. Listen for the **short u** sound \ŭ\ as in *gum*. Color the picture if its name has the short *u* sound.

Introducing the short *u* sound \ŭ\.

www.summerbridgeactivities.com   Phonics Connection---Grade 1—RBP0237

Uu

Look at the letters in the rubber band. Stretch out the sounds; then snap them together to make the word. Say "s—" "u—" "n—" "sun." Print the word.

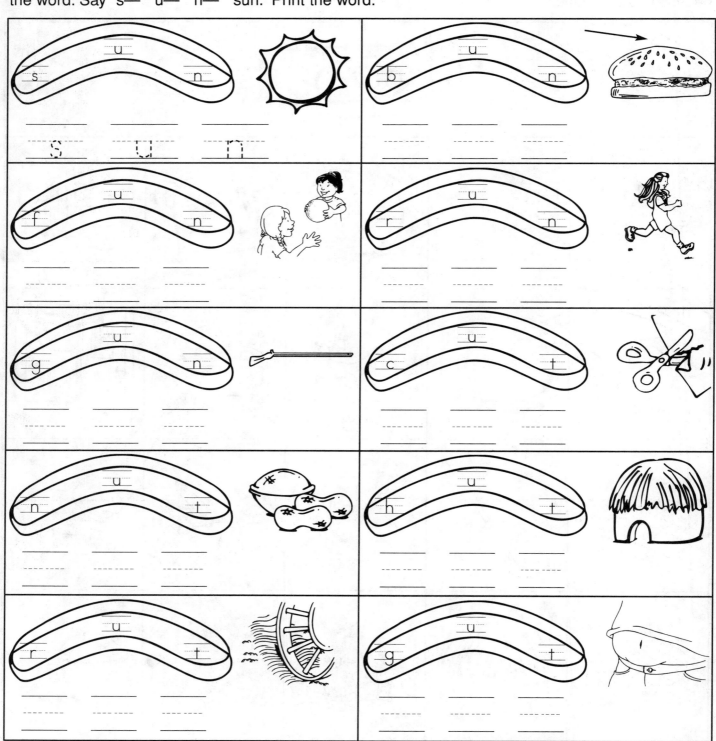

s u n

s u n

www.summerbridgeactivities.com   ©RBP Books

Name _____

Uu

Look at the letters in the rubber band. Stretch out the sounds; then snap them together to make the word. Say "c—" "u—" "p—" "cup." Print the word. Draw a line from the word to the picture.

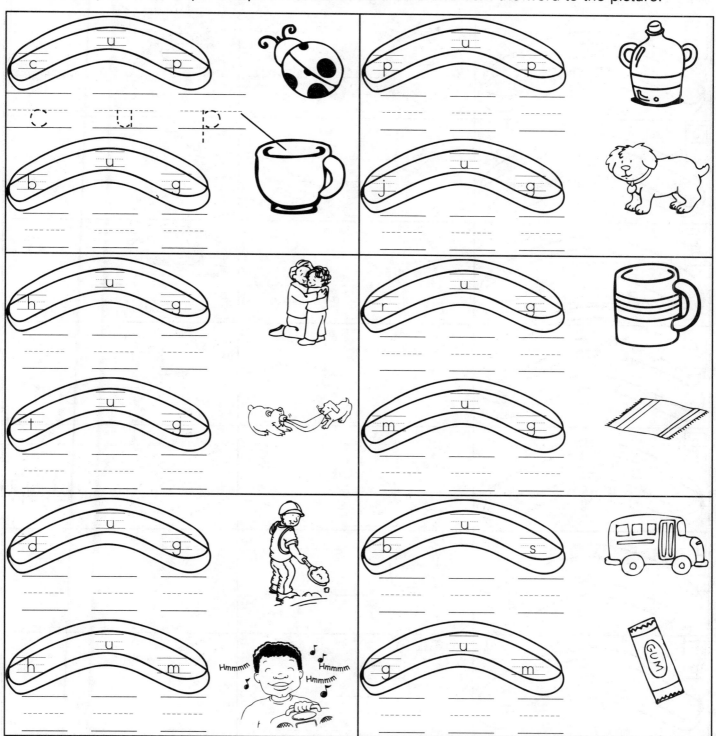

Using the sound of short *u*; word chunks *up*, *ug*, *us*, and *um*.

www.summerbridgeactivities.com

55

Phonics Connection—Grade 1—RBP0237

Uu

Look at the letters in the rubber band. Stretch out the sounds; then snap them together to make the word. Say "r—" "u—" "b—" "rub." Add the beginning sound from the box to make a word. Print the word.

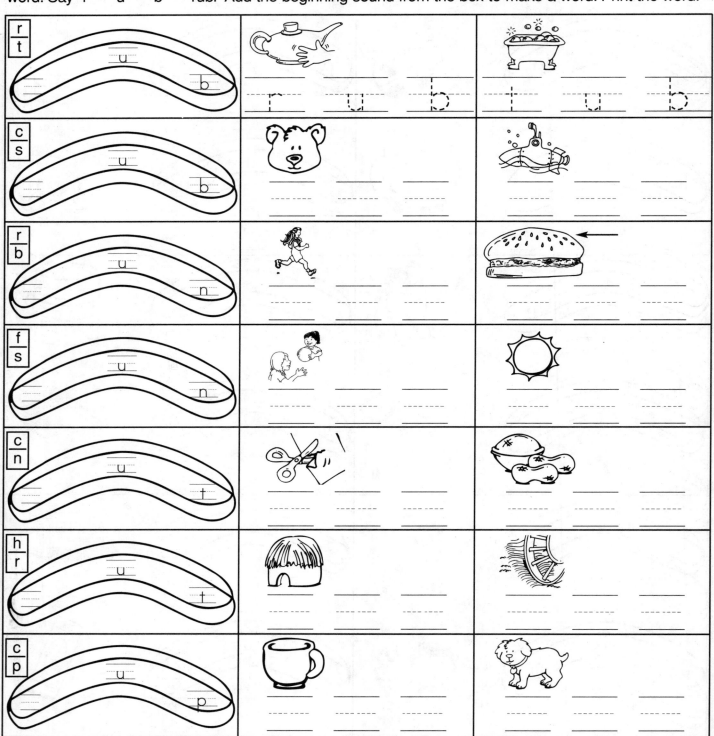

Using the sound of short *u*; word chunks *up*, *ub*, *ut*, and *un*.

www.summerbridgeactivities.com

©RBP Books

Name _____

Uu

Look at the letters in the rubber band. Stretch out the sounds; then snap them together to make the word. Say "b—" "u—" "g—" "bug." Add the ending chunk from the box to make a word. Print the word.

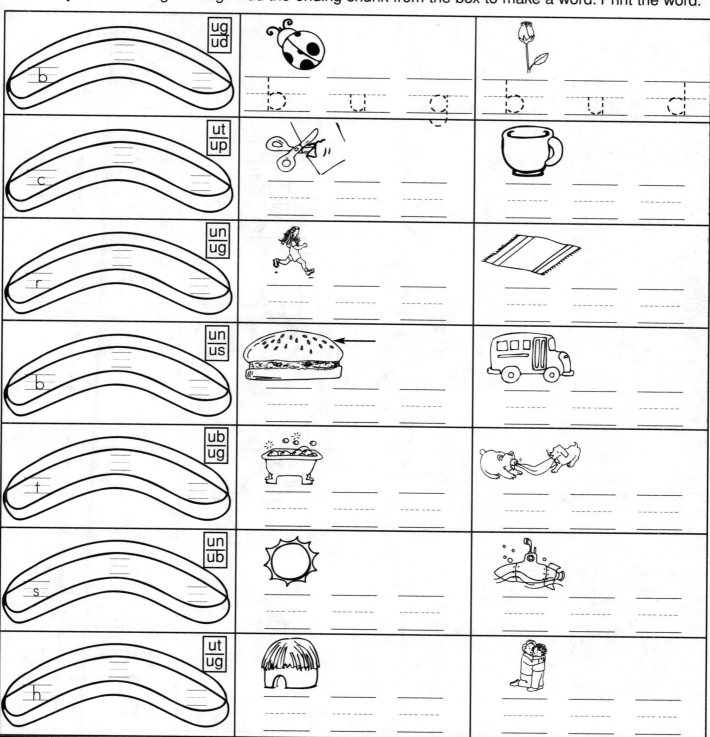

Using the sound of short *u*; word chunks *ub*, *un*, *up*, *ug*, *ut*, and *us*.

Phonics Connection—Grade 1—RBP0237

Uu

Say each picture name. Listen for the **short *u*** sound \ŭ\. Print the *u* where you hear the short *u* sound.

b __u__ g	j __ g	h __ g	r __ g
t __ g	m __ g	b __ s	m __ d
b __ d	s __ b	h __ m	g __ m
s __ m	r __ b	t __ b	c __ b
h __ t	h __ b	r __ n	b __ n

Using the sound of short *u*; word chunks *ud*, *ug*, *us*, *ub*, *un*, *ut*, and *um*.

58

Uu

Say each picture name. Listen for the sounds. Print the word.

f u n

Using the sound of short *u*; word chunks *up*, *ug*, *us*, *ub*, *un*, *ut*, and *um*.

www.summerbridgeactivities.com   Phonics Connection—Grade 1—RBP0237

Name

Uu

Say each picture name. Listen to each sound. Fill in the bubble for the correct word. Print the word for the picture.

○ cap	
○ pup	
● cup	

cup

| ○ rug |
| ○ bug |
| ○ rig |

| ○ tub |
| ○ tab |
| ○ tug |

| ○ sub |
| ○ cub |
| ○ tag |

| ○ hat |
| ○ hut |
| ○ sun |

| ○ run |
| ○ bun |
| ○ ham |

| ○ gum |
| ○ hug |
| ○ hat |

| ○ mix |
| ○ bud |
| ○ cub |

| ○ fin |
| ○ fun |
| ○ cut |

| ○ nut |
| ○ big |
| ○ dug |

| ○ rib |
| ○ bus |
| ○ rub |

| ○ ram |
| ○ run |
| ○ bun |

Using the sound of short *u* word chunks; standardized testing form.

Name

Uu

Game with **short _u_** words. Begin the game at the word _Start_. Toss a die to determine how many squares you can move. Say the word you land on. If you can not say the word, go back one space. The one who lands on _Finish_ first wins.

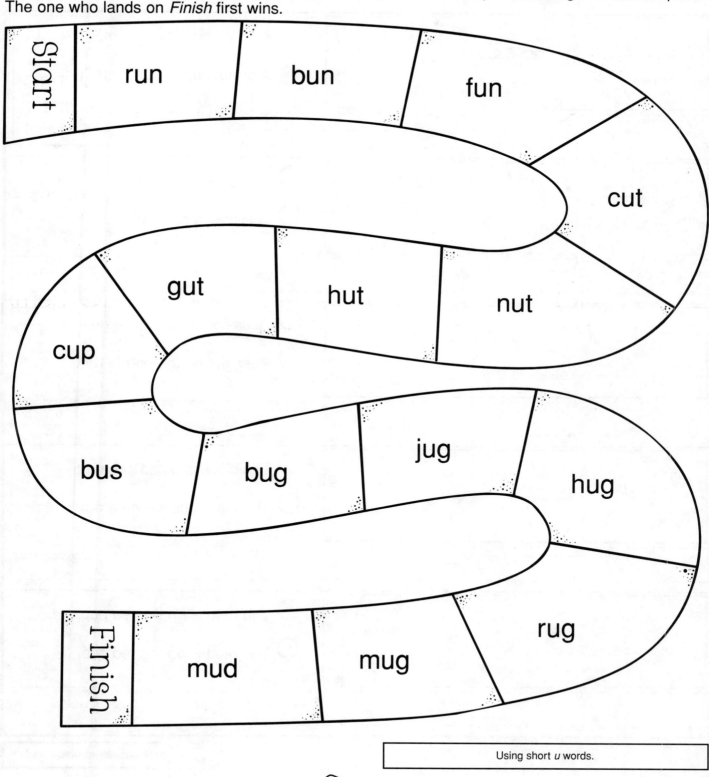

Using short _u_ words.

www.summerbridgeactivities.com

Phonics Connection—Grade 1—RBP0237

Name

Uu

Read each sentence. Listen to each sound. Fill in one bubble. Then print that sentence. Draw a picture of that sentence.

| | ○ A green bug sat on a mug. |
| | ● A green bug sat on a tub. |

A green bug sat on a tub.

| | ○ Gus saw a blue nut. |
| | ○ Gus saw a blue hut. |

| | ○ Russ sat in the purple gum. |
| | ○ Russ sat on the purple rug. |

| | ○ The black cub can dig a rut. |
| | ○ The black cub sat on a nut. |

| | ○ The mud is on the red pup. |
| | ○ The mud is on the red bus. |

Recognizing short *u* words.

Phonics Connection—Grade 1—RBP0237   www.summerbridgeactivities.com   ©RBP Books

Name _____

Uu

Read each sentence. Print a word that rhymes with the underlined word. Make the sentence tell about the picture to the right.

1. Gus had <u>fun</u> in the sun.

2. <u>Bud</u> got in the _____

3. A <u>bug</u> is on the _____

4. Russ fed the <u>pup</u> with a _____

5. The cub can <u>tug</u> on the _____

6. I had a <u>nut</u> in the _____

7. Sam will <u>rub</u> the _____

8. The man <u>cut</u> a _____

Using language arts; using context clues to select rhyming words with short *u* word chunks.

www.summerbridgeactivities.com Phonics Connection—Grade 1—RBP0237

Name

Uu

Read each sentence. Read the three words. Look at the picture. Fill in the bubble next to the word that makes sense in the sentence. Print the word on the line.

1. Bud has a big cub̲ ̲ ̲ ̲ .

● cub
○ cut
○ cat

2. Russ had a ̲ ̲ ̲ ̲ ̲ .

○ hut
○ nut
○ hit

3. Gus can run to the ̲ ̲ ̲ ̲ .

○ tub
○ bus
○ sun

4. Jim ate a bun in the ̲ ̲ ̲ ̲ .

○ sun
○ jug
○ tub

5. The hut was on the ̲ ̲ ̲ ̲ .

○ mud
○ sub
○ gum

6. Tug can ̲ ̲ ̲ ̲ for us.

○ hum
○ fun
○ jug

Using language arts; using context clues to select missing words with short *u* word chunks.

Phonics Connection—Grade 1—RBP0237   www.summerbridgeactivities.com   ©RBP Books

Uu

Read the words. Look at the picture. Write the words in the correct order to match the picture.

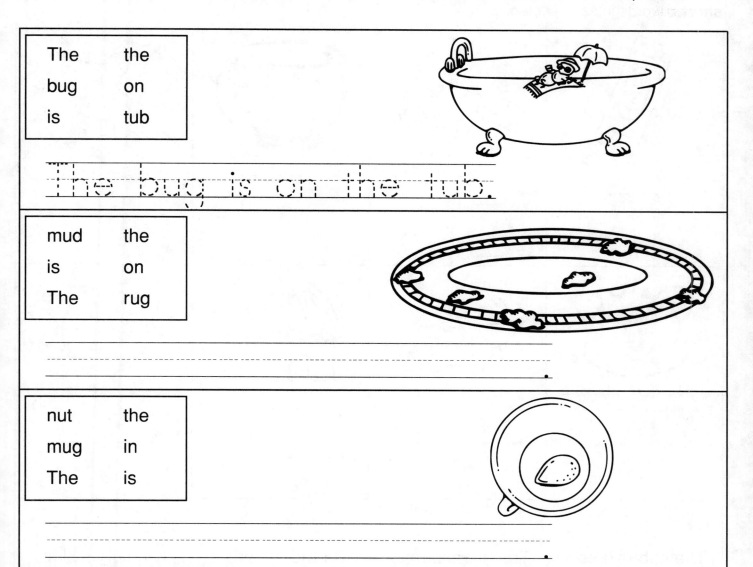

The	the
bug	on
is	tub

The bug is on the tub.

mud	the
is	on
The	rug

_____ .

nut	the
mug	in
The	is

_____ .

the	sub
cub	in
is	The

_____ .

Using language arts; using context clues to write sentences; using short *u* words.

Uu

Write the name of the picture. Read the sentences below and color each picture. Underline the **short u** words in each sentence.

gum _____

The cub is green.   The nut is purple.   The hut is red.   The sub is blue.

The pup is red.   The sun is yellow.   The cup is green.   The gum is blue.

Language arts application; short u word chunks up, ut, ub, un, and um.

Name

Uu

Read the story below. Say each word. Listen carefully for the **short _u_** sound \ŭ\. Draw a line under each word with the short _u_ sound. Draw pictures of what is happening in the story as you read it.

"Kim's <u>pup</u> is bad," said <u>Bud</u> to <u>Gus</u>.

"He tugs on rugs.

He bats at bugs.

He tips mugs.

He digs in the mud.

He is a bad pup.

He hid my gum!"

"He is not bad," said Gus.

"He is a fun pup, and fun pups dig and tug."

"This is not fun. I want my gum," said Bud.

Read the story once more. Read the questions below. Fill in the bubble by the correct answer.

1. Is Bud a pup?   no ◯   yes ◯

2. Is the pup bad?   no ◯   yes ◯

3. Did the pup dig in the mud?   no ◯   yes ◯

4. Did the pup tug on rugs?   no ◯   yes ◯

Write a title for the story. _____

_____

Tell a friend what might happen next in the story.

Name

Oo

Say each picture name. Listen for the **short *o*** sound \ŏ\ as in *log*. Color the picture if its name has the short *o* sound.

Introducing the short *o* sound \ŏ\.

www.summerbridgeactivities.com

Oo

Look at the letters in the rubber band. Stretch out the sounds; then snap them together to make the word. Say "p—" "o—" "t—" "pot." Print the word. Draw a line from the word to the picture.

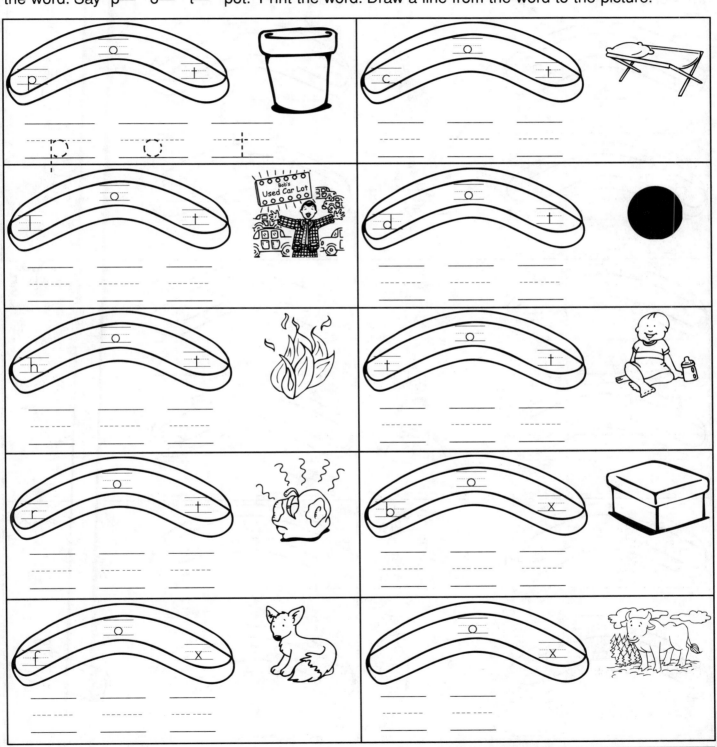

Using the sound of short *o* word chunks *ot* and *ox*.

© RBP Books   www.summerbridgeactivities.com   Phonics Connection—Grade 1—RBP0237

Oo

Look at the letters in the rubber band. Stretch out the sounds; then snap them together to make the word. Say "t—" "o—" "p—" "top." Print the word. Draw a line from the word to the picture.

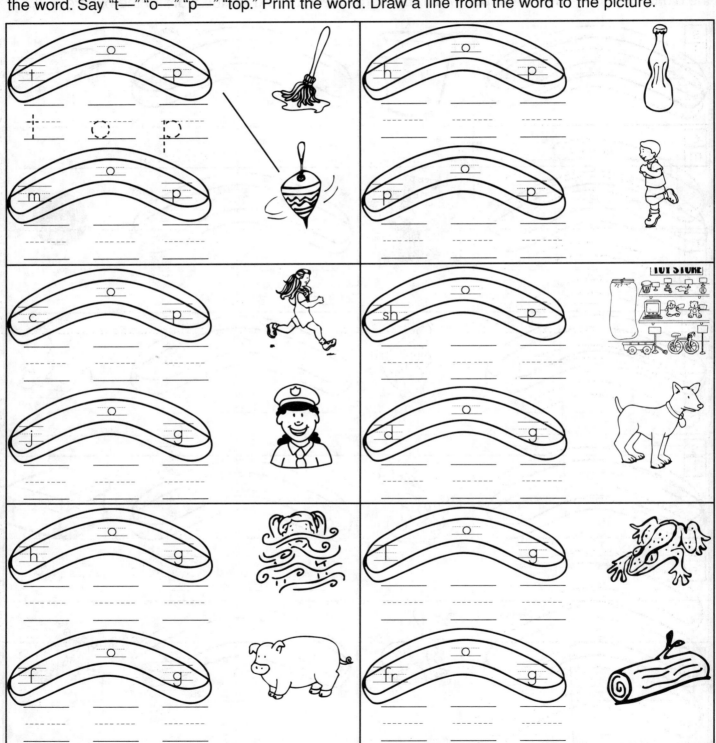

t o p	h o p
t o p	
m o p	p o p
c o p	sh o p
j o g	d o g
h o g	l o g
f o g	fr o g

Using the sound of short *o*; word chunks *op* and *og*.

Oo

Look at the letters in the rubber band. Stretch out the sounds; then snap them together to make the word. Say "s—" "o—" "b—" "sob." Add the beginning sound from the box to make a word. Print the word.

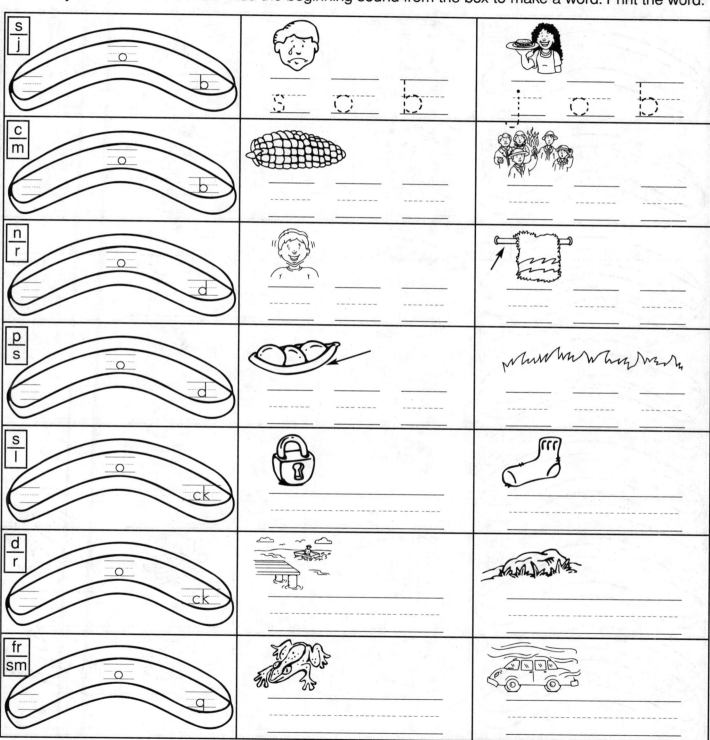

Using the sound of short *o*; word chunks *og*, *od*, *ob*, and *ock*.

Name

Oo

Look at the letters in the rubber band. Stretch out the sounds; then snap them together to make the word. Say "p—" "o—" "t—" "pot." Add the ending chunk from the box to make a word. Print the word.

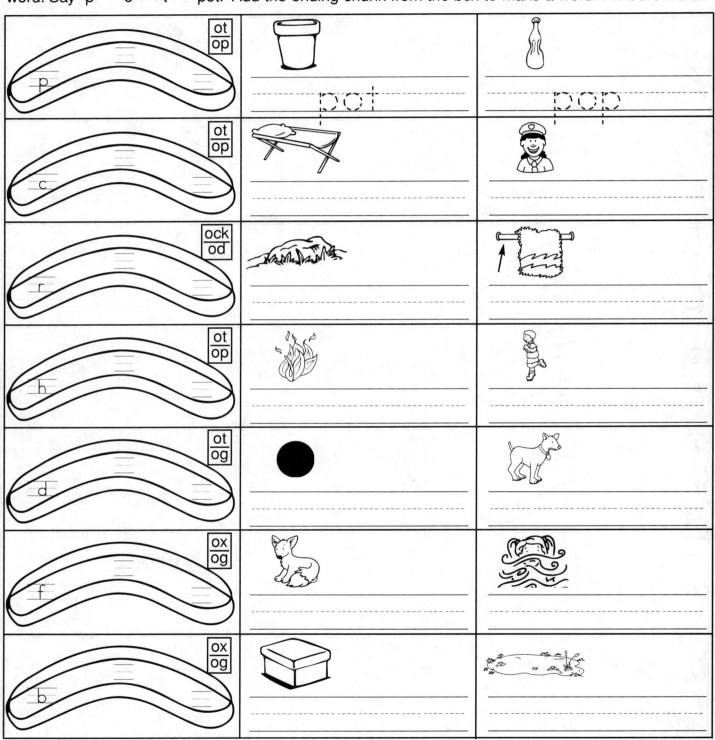

p — ot / op	pot	pop
c — ot / op		
r — ock / od		
h — ot / op		
d — ot / og		
f — ox / og		
b — ox / og		

Using the sound of short *o*; word chunks *op*, *og*, *ot*, *ox*, *od*, and *ock*.

www.summerbridgeactivities.com

Name

Oo

Say each picture name. Listen for the **short o** sound \ŏ\. Print the *o* when you hear the short *o* sound.

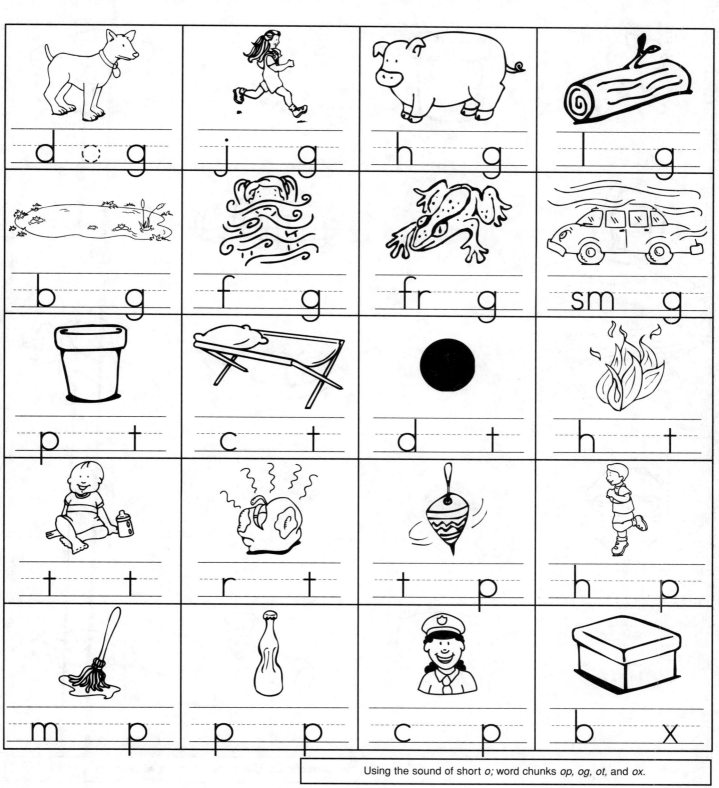

d o g	j _ g	h _ g	l _ g
b _ g	f _ g	fr _ g	sm _ g
p _ t	c _ t	d _ t	h _ t
t _ t	r _ t	t _ p	h _ p
m _ p	p _ p	c _ p	b _ x

Using the sound of short *o*; word chunks *op*, *og*, *ot*, and *ox*.

www.summerbridgeactivities.com **Phonics Connection—Grade 1—RBP0237**

Oo

Say each picture name. Listen for the sounds. Print the word.

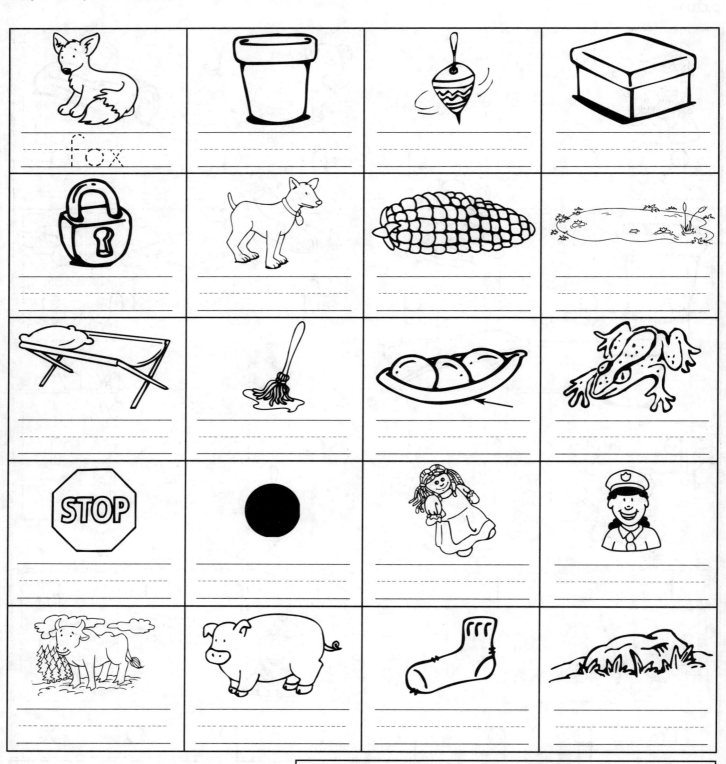

fox

Using the sound of short *o*; word chunks *op, og, ot, ox, od, ob,* and *ock.*

Phonics Connection—Grade 1—RBP0237

www.summerbridgeactivities.com

©RBP Books

Name _____

Oo

Say each picture name. Listen to each sound. Fill in the correct bubble. Print the word for the picture.

● cop ○ cap ○ cup	○ job ○ cob ○ cab	○ rid ○ rot ○ rod
cop		
○ pot ○ pat ○ pit	○ hat ○ hot ○ hut	○ box ○ fix ○ bag
○ hog ○ hut ○ hat	○ mix ○ mop ○ mud	○ fin ○ fun ○ fox
○ nut ○ big ○ dog	○ rib ○ bus ○ rob	○ ram ○ run ○ rock

Using the sound of short *o* word chunks; standardized testing form.

 75

Oo

Game with **short *o*** words. Begin the game at the word *Start*. Toss a die to determine how many squares you can move. Say the word you land on. If you can not say the word, go back one space. The one who lands on *Finish* first wins.

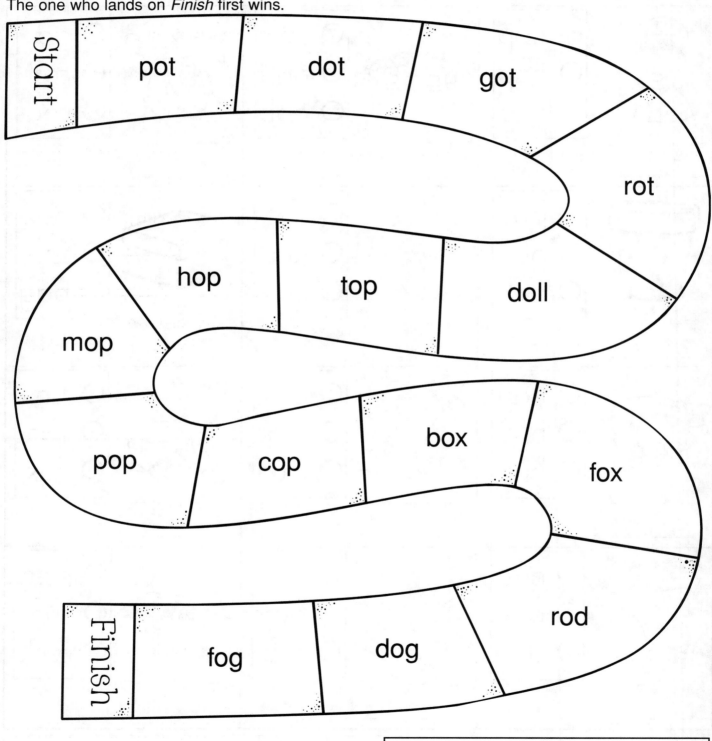

Start

pot

dot

got

rot

hop

top

doll

mop

pop

cop

box

fox

rod

Finish

fog

dog

Using short *o* word chunks.

www.summerbridgeactivities.com

Name

Oo

Read each sentence. Listen to each sound. Fill in one bubble. Print that sentence. Draw a picture of that sentence.

● The red fox ran at the dog.
○ The red fox will hop in a box.

The red fox ran at the dog.

○ A pink hog bit a cob.
○ A pink hog bit a frog.

○ Rod had a blue sock
○ Rod had a blue top.

○ Dot got a purple cot.
○ Dot got a purple log.

○ Ron hid a pot in the blue box.
○ Ron hid a mop in the blue box.

Recognizing short o words.

© RBP Books   www.summerbridgeactivities.com   Phonics Connection—Grade 1—RBP0237

Name

Oo

Read each sentence. Print a word that rhymes with the underlined word. Make the sentence tell about the picture to the right.

1. The <u>fox</u> is in the box _____.

2. A <u>hog</u> sat in a _____.

3. I will not <u>jog</u> in the _____.

4. The <u>pot</u> is _____.

5. The <u>frog</u> is on the _____.

6. The <u>cot</u> has a _____.

7. Ron and the <u>cop</u> can _____.

8. Rod had to <u>stop</u> at the _____.

Using language arts; using context clues to select rhyming words with short *o* word chunks.

Phonics Connection—Grade 1—RBP0237   www.summerbridgeactivities.com   ©RBP Books

Oo

Read each sentence. Read the three words. Look at the picture. Fill in the bubble next to the word that makes sense in the sentence. Print the word on the line.

1. Dot can hop like a ~~frog~~ .	● frog ○ log ○ bat	
2. Ron put the doll in a _____ .	○ box ○ bib ○ hat	
3. John got the _____ for his mom.	○ mop ○ bus ○ bag	
4. The tot can draw _____ .	○ dots ○ hogs ○ tops	
5. The fox hid in the _____ .	○ mud ○ sub ○ log	
6. Todd can do a good _____ .	○ job ○ jog ○ song	

Using language arts; using context clues to select missing words with short *o* word chunks.

Name

Oo

Read the words. Look at the picture. Write the words in the correct order to match the picture.

The	the
fox	on
is	box

The box is on the fox.

cop	the
is	on
The	pop

_____ _____ _____ _____ _____ _____ .

dog	the
fog	in
The	is

_____ _____ _____ _____ _____ _____ .

the	tot
cot	on
is	The

_____ _____ _____ _____ _____ _____ .

Using language arts; using context clues to write sentences; word chunks *op, og, ot,* and *ox.*

Name

Oo

Write the name of the picture. Read the sentences below and color each picture. Underline the **short o** words in each sentence.

pot

The pot is green.   The cot is purple.   The mop is red.   The top is blue.

The frog is red.   The dog is yellow.   The log is green.   The hog is blue.

Language arts application; short o word chunks op, og, and ot.

© RBP Books   www.summerbridgeactivities.com   Phonics Connection—Grade 1—RBP0237

Oo

Read the story below. Say each word. Listen carefully for the **short *o*** sound \ŏ\. Draw a line under each word with the short *o* sound. Draw pictures of what is happening in the story as you read it.

A <u>frog</u> sat <u>on</u> a <u>log</u> by the <u>pond</u>.

Along came a dog.

The dog sat on the log.

The dog sang a song.

The frog did not like the song.

The frog hopped off the log.

Along came a hog.

The hog sat on the log.

The dog sang a song.

The hog did not like the song.

The hog popped off the log.

Read the story once more. Read the questions below. Fill in the bubble by the correct answer.

1. Did the frog sing a song first?   no ◯   yes ◯

2. Did the frog like the song?   no ◯   yes ◯

3. Did the hog like the song?   no ◯   yes ◯

4. How did the frog get off the log?

5. How did the hog get off the log?

Write a title for the story.

Tell a friend what might happen next in the story.

Language arts application; reading and answering comprehension questions with short *o* word chunks.

Name

Ee

Say each picture name. Listen for the **short** *e* sound \ĕ\ as in *jet*. Color the picture if its name has the short *e* sound.

Introducing the short e sound \ĕ\.

www.summerbridgeactivities.com   Phonics Connection—Grade 1—RBP0237

Name

Ee

Look at the letters in the rubber band. Stretch out the sounds; then snap them together to make the word. Say "p—" "e—" "t—" "pet." Print the word.

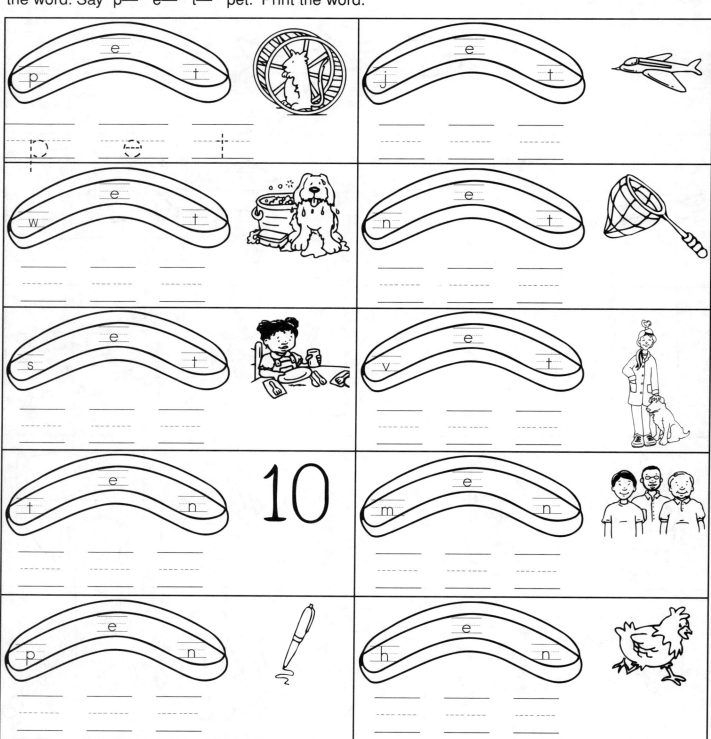

p   e   t

p e t

j   e   t

w   e   t

n   e   t

s   e   t

v   e   t

t   e   n

10

m   e   n

p   e   n

h   e   n

Using the sound of short *e*; word chunks *et* and *en*.

Ee

Look at the letters in the rubber band. Stretch out the sounds; then snap them together to make the word. Say "b—" "e—" "d—" "bed." Print the word. Draw a line from the word to the picture.

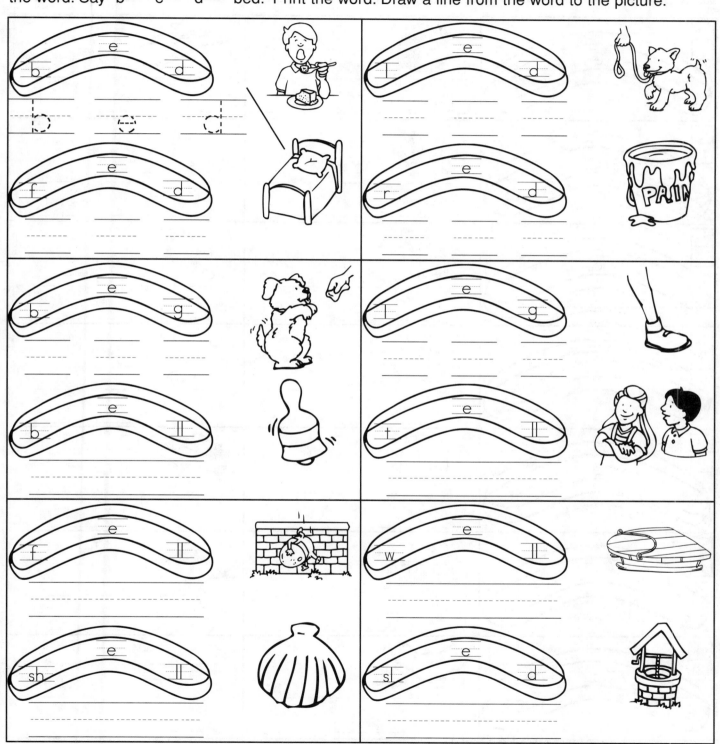

Using the sound of short *e*; word chunks *ed*, *ell*, and *eg*.

www.summerbridgeactivities.com

Phonics Connection—Grade 1—RBP0237

Name

Ee

Look at the letters in the rubber band. Stretch out the sounds; then snap them together to make the word. Say "p—" "e—" "t—" "pet." Add the beginning sound from the box to make a word. Print the word.

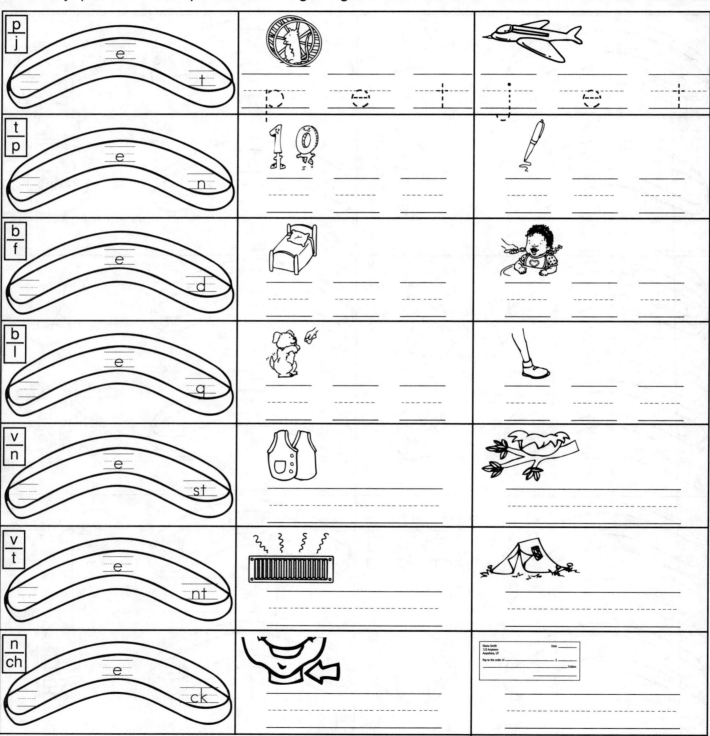

p / j   e   t

t / p   e   n

b / f   e   d

b / l   e   g

v / n   e   st

v / t   e   nt

n / ch   e   ck

Using the sound of short *e*; word chunks *et, en, ent, ed, est, eck,* and *eg*.

Name

Ee

Look at the letters in the rubber band. Stretch out the sounds; then snap them together to make the word. Say "p—" "e—" "t—" "pet." Add the ending chunk from the box to make a word. Print the word.

p **et** / **en**	 p e t	p e n
h **en** / **em**		
w **et** / **eb**		
b **eg** / **ed**		
l **ed** / **eg**		
f **ell** / **ed**		
m **et** / **en**		

Using the sound of short *e*; word chunks *et, en, eb, ed, eb, em, ell, em,* and *eg*.

www.summerbridgeactivities.com **Phonics Connection—Grade 1—RBP0237**

Name

Ee

Say each picture name. Listen for the **short e** sound \ĕ\. Print the *e* when you hear the short e sound.

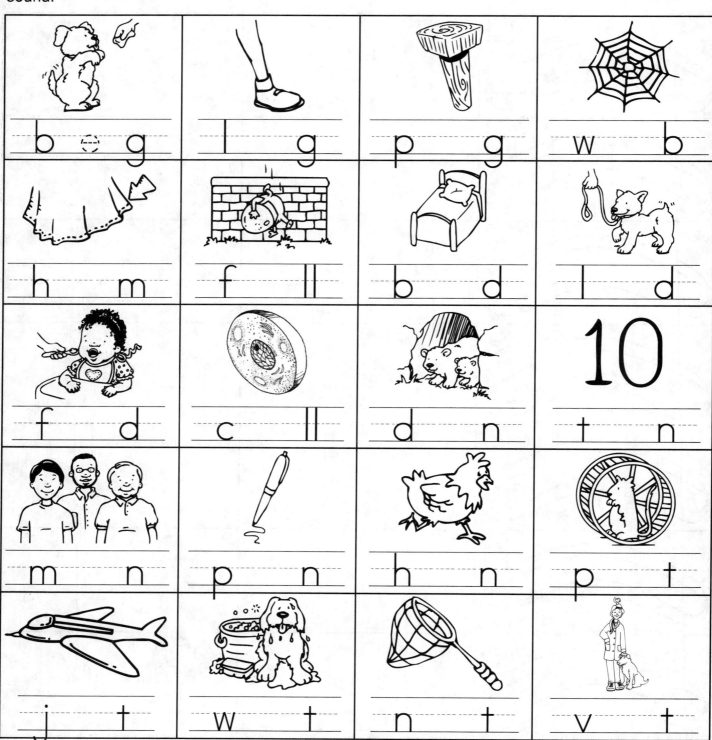

b ⊙ g	l _ g	p _ g	w _ b
h _ m	f _ ll	b _ d	l _ d
f _ d	c _ ll	d _ n	t _ n
m _ n	p _ n	h _ n	p _ t
j _ t	w _ t	n _ t	v _ t

Using the sound of short e word chunks *eb*, *em*, *et*, *en*, *ed*, *ell*, and *eg*.

Name

Ee

Say each picture name. Listen for the sounds. Print the word.

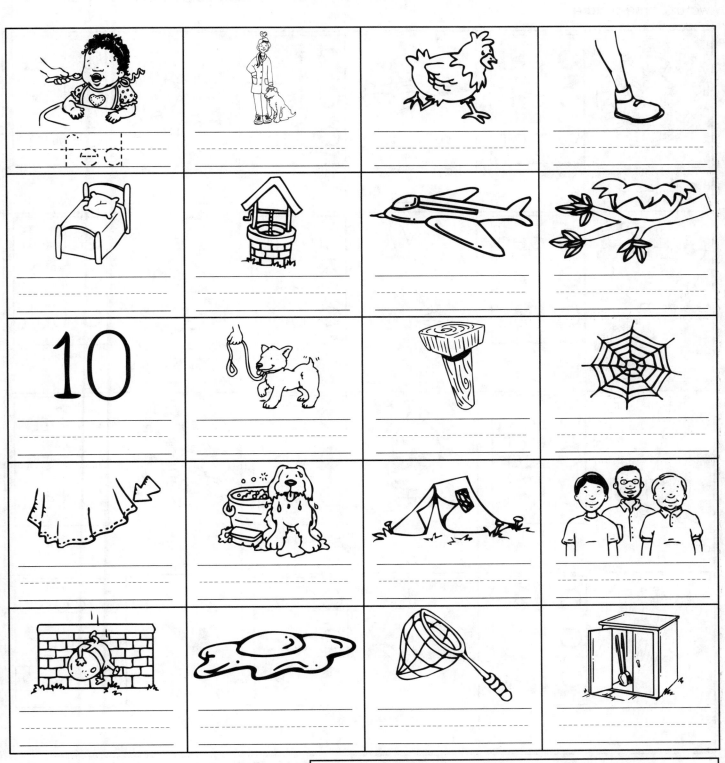

Using the sound of short *e* word chunks *et, en, ed, ell, est, eb, em, ent,* and *eg.*

©RBP Books   www.summerbridgeactivities.com   **Phonics Connection—Grade 1—RBP0237**

Ee

Say each picture name. Listen to each sound. Fill in the bubble for the correct word. Then print the word for the picture.

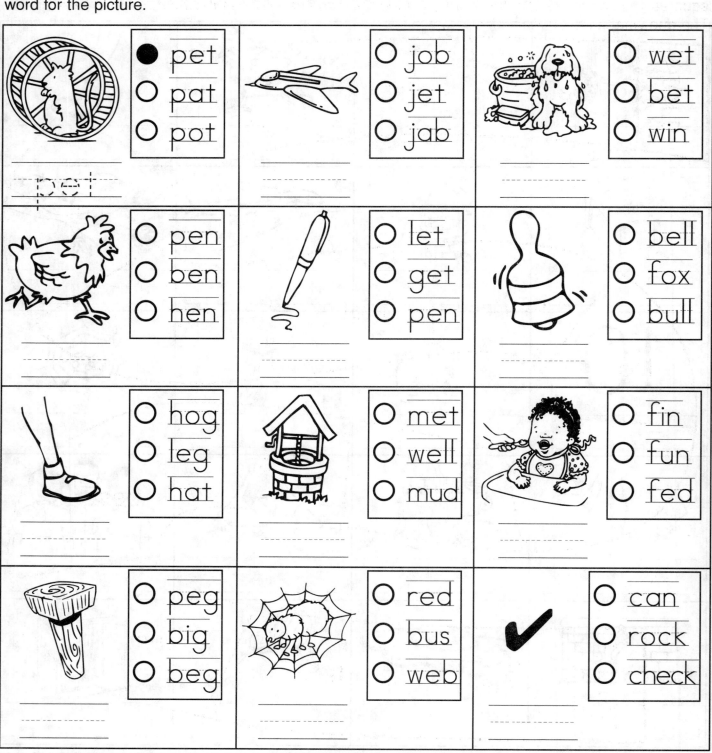

Picture	Choices	Write
(hamster on wheel)	● pet ○ pat ○ pot	pet
(jet)	○ job ○ jet ○ jab	
(wet dog)	○ wet ○ bet ○ win	
(hen)	○ pen ○ ben ○ hen	
(pen)	○ let ○ get ○ pen	
(bell)	○ bell ○ fox ○ bull	
(leg)	○ hog ○ leg ○ hat	
(well)	○ met ○ well ○ mud	
(baby being fed)	○ fin ○ fun ○ fed	
(peg)	○ peg ○ big ○ beg	
(web with spider)	○ red ○ bus ○ web	
(check mark)	○ can ○ rock ○ check	

Using the sound of short *e* word chunks; standardized testing form.

Name

Ee

Game with **short _e_** words. Begin the game at the word _Start_. Toss a die to determine how many squares you can move. Say the word you land on. If you can not say the word, go back one space. The one who lands on _Finish_ first wins.

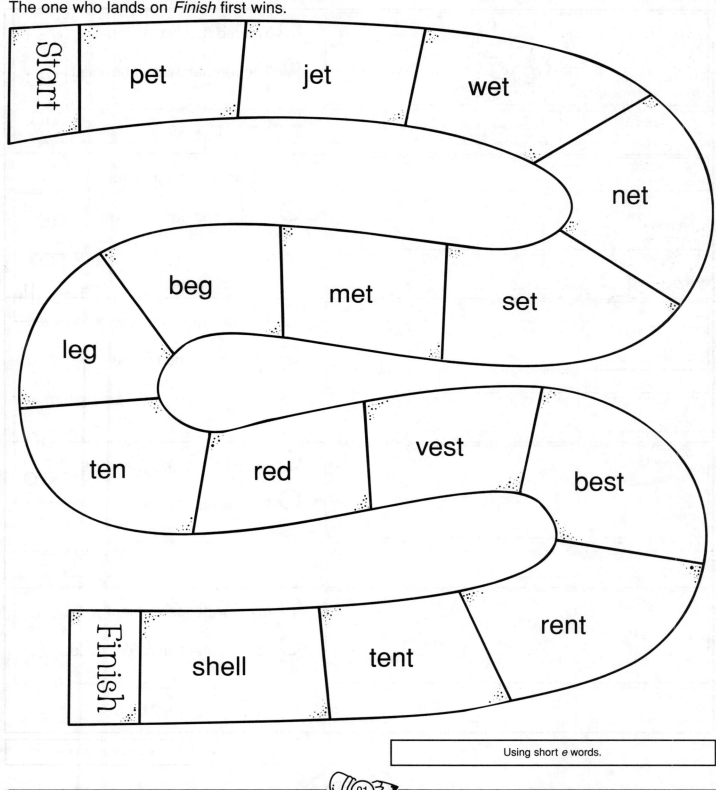

Using short _e_ words.

© RBP Books www.summerbridgeactivities.com Phonics Connection—Grade 1—RBP0237

Name

Ee

Read each sentence. Listen to each sound. Fill in the bubble for one sentence. Print that sentence. Draw a picture of that sentence.

○ The red hen was in a pen

● The red hen was in her nest.

The red hen was in her nest.

○ A blue dog ran to a vet.

○ A blue dog had on a vest.

○ Rod fed the hen in the green shed.

○ Rod fed the dog in the green shed.

○ Ben can get on a white jet.

○ Ben has a white tent.

○ My new pet can sit in a web.

○ My new pet can sit on a bed.

Recognizing short *e* words.

Phonics Connection—Grade 1—RBP0237   www.summerbridgeactivities.com   ©RBP Books

Ee

Read each sentence. Print a word that rhymes with the underlined word. Make the sentence tell about the picture to the right.

1. The bird sat in her <u>nest</u> for a rest .

2. The <u>pet</u> dog went to the _____ .

3. Ben had <u>ten</u> big, fat _____

4. Deb had a <u>sled</u> under the _____

5. Meg <u>fell</u> in the _____

6. The <u>pet</u> got _____

7. Yeta was to <u>tell</u> about her _____

8. The <u>men</u> went into the bear _____

Using language arts; using context clues to select rhyming words with short *e* word chunks.

©RBP Books   www.summerbridgeactivities.com   Phonics Connection—Grade 1—RBP0237

Name

Ee

Read each sentence. Read the three words. Look at the picture. Fill in the bubble next to the word that makes sense in the sentence. Print the word on the line.

1.	The vet can help the ___hen.___	● hen ○ log ○ tent	*(chicken)*
2.	Meg set the rat on the _____	○ bib ○ bed ○ hat	*(bed)*
3.	The men will get on a _____	○ jet ○ bus ○ bag	*(jet)*
4.	Ted hit his leg on the _____	○ dot ○ hog ○ peg	*(peg)*
5.	The bear hid in the _____	○ mud ○ den ○ web	*(den)*
6.	At the shop Bev got a _____	○ job ○ shell ○ song	*(shell)*

Using language arts; using context clues to select missing words with short *e* word chunks.

www.summerbridgeactivities.com   ©**RBP Books**

Ee

Read the words. Look at the picture. Write the words in the correct order to match the picture.

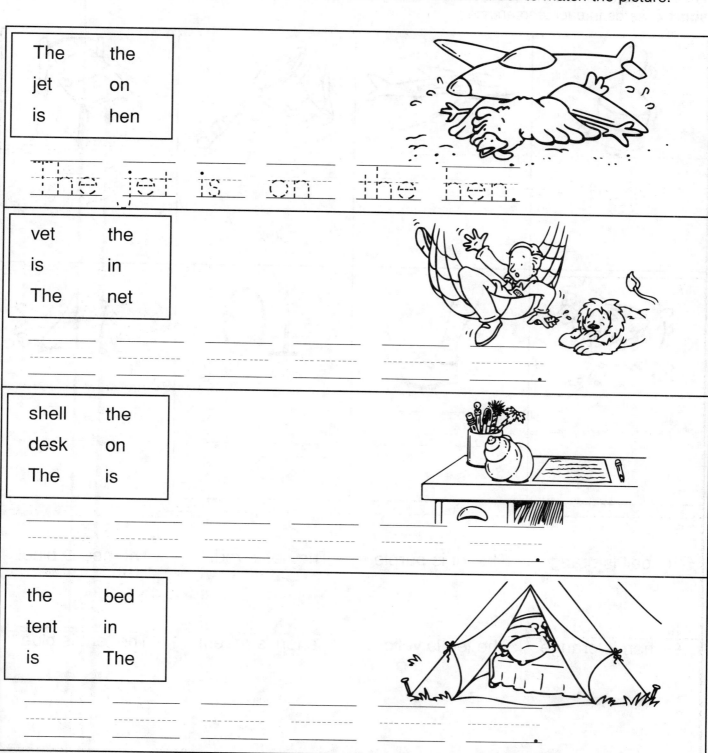

The	the
jet	on
is	hen

The jet is on the hen.

vet	the
is	in
The	net

shell	the
desk	on
The	is

the	bed
tent	in
is	The

Using language arts; using context clues to write sentences; word chunks *et, en, ed, ent,* and *ell.*

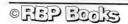

Name

Ee

Write the name of the picture. Read each sentence below and color each picture. Underline the **short e** words in each sentence.

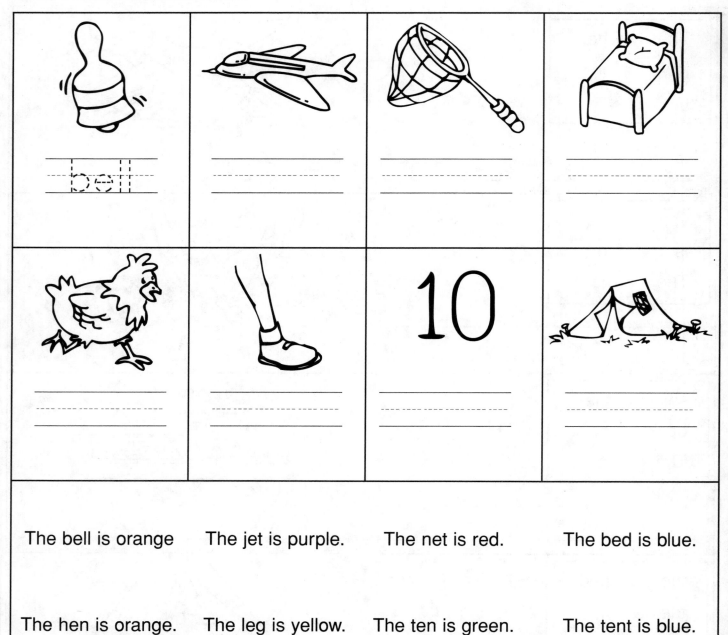

bell	_____	_____	_____
_____	_____	_____	_____

The bell is orange   The jet is purple.   The net is red.   The bed is blue.

The hen is orange.   The leg is yellow.   The ten is green.   The tent is blue.

Language arts application; short e word chunks et, en, ed, ell, and eg.

Phonics Connection—Grade 1—RBP0237   www.summerbridgeactivities.com   © RBP Books

Name

Ee

Read the story below. Say each word. Listen carefully for the **short e** sound \ĕ\. Draw a line under each word with the short *e* sound. Draw pictures of what is happening in the story as you read it.

Ben has a hen.
The hen has ten chicks.
The hen and her chicks
are in a pen.
Tim fed the hen and her
chicks red pellets.

The hen did not feel well.
Ben took the hen to the
vet.
Vets help pets get well.
The vet told Ben how to
help the hen.
He said, "Give her a nest
and a lot of rest."

Read the story once more. Read the questions below. Fill in the bubble by the correct answer.

1. Is the hen in a pen?   no ◯   yes ◯

2. Did the hen feel well?   no ◯   yes ◯

3. What do you think will happen to the hen?

4. Who will feed the chicks?

Write a title for the story.

Tell a friend what might happen next in the story.

Language arts application; reading and answering comprehension questions with short *e* word chunks.

97

Name

Aa

Say each picture name. Listen for the **long** *a* sound \ā\ as in *train*. Color the picture if its name has the long *a* sound.

Introducing the long *a* sound \ā\.

Aa

Say each picture name. Listen for the *a* vowel sound. Print ā if you hear the long *a* sound or ă if you hear the short *a* sound.

ā

ă

Using the sound of long *a* and short *a*.

Name

Aa

cāke̸

Say each picture name. Listen for the **long a** vowel sound \ā\. Print the word for the picture name.
Rule: In a word that has two vowels, and one is final *e*, the first vowel is long and the *e* is silent.

can cane	cap cape	mad made	lamb lame
c̄an̸e̸			
man mane	pan pane	mat mate	fat fate
van vane	tap tape	land lane	rat rate
nap nape	dam dame	fad fade	hat hate

Using the sound of long *a* word chunks with _a_e.

Aa

p̄aint

Say each picture name. Listen for the vowel sound. Print the word for the picture name.

Rule: In a word where two vowels are together, the first vowel usually is long and the second is silent.

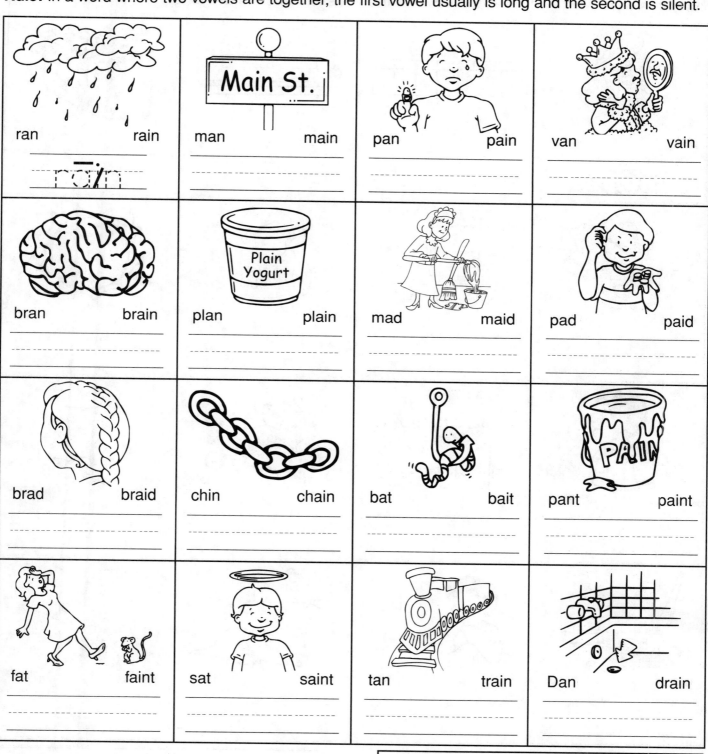

ran	rain	man	main	pan	pain	van	vain

rain

bran	brain	plan	plain	mad	maid	pad	paid

brad	braid	chin	chain	bat	bait	pant	paint

fat	faint	sat	saint	tan	train	Dan	drain

Using the sound of long *a*; word chunks with *ai*.

Name

Aa

hāy

Say each picture name. Listen for the vowel sound. Print the word for the picture name.
Rule: In a word where *y* follows the vowel *a*, the *y* is silent and the *a* is long.

bat bay	dam day	tab tray	hat hay
bāy			
lad lay	mad May	pat pay	rat ray
sat say	wag way	clam clay	jab jay
grass gray	plan pray	stamp stay	pan play

Using the sound of long *a*; word chunk *ay*.

www.summerbridgeactivities.com

Aa

cake **cāke**   maid **māid**   hay **hāy**

Say each picture name. Listen for the vowel sound. Print the word for the picture.

tape

c   v   c   p   p   n

g   m   m   n   b   t   p   n

c   n   w   v   r   n   r   y

p   y   d   y   h   y   b   y

Using the sound of long a; word chunks _a_e, _ai_, _ay.

(103)

Aa

Say each picture name. Listen for the vowel sound. Fill in the bubble for the picture word, and then print the word.

○ pan ○ pane ● page	○ cage ○ can ○ came	○ tap ○ tape ○ tame	○ fane ○ fan ○ fat
○ tack ○ take ○ tan	○ date ○ dam ○ dame	○ laid ○ lake ○ lane	○ back ○ bait ○ bat
○ sat ○ saint ○ sage	○ rage ○ rag ○ rake	○ mane ○ man ○ mat	○ pat ○ paint ○ pain
○ sake ○ snake ○ sack	○ mat ○ mate ○ main	○ train ○ tran ○ strain	○ ape ○ cape ○ scrape

Using the sound of long *a*; spelling with *a* word chunks; standardized testing form.

Name

Aa

Read each sentence. Read the three words. Look at the picture. Fill in the bubble next to the word that makes sense in the sentence. Print the word on the line.

1. Dan _ate_ the cake.

- ● ate
- ○ at
- ○ gate

2. Is the bat in the _____ ?

- ○ case
- ○ cave
- ○ can

3. Dad put the _____ into the box.

- ○ mat
- ○ maid
- ○ may

4. Sue will _____ the game.

- ○ play
- ○ page
- ○ make

5. Jim will _____ the grass.

- ○ rake
- ○ rat
- ○ rage

6. At the shop Bev got a _____ .

- ○ came
- ○ cage
- ○ cave

Using language arts; using context clues to select missing words with the *a* sound.

105

Name

Aa

Read the story below. Say each word. Listen carefully for the **long** *a* sound \ā\. Draw a line under each word with the long *a* sound. Draw pictures of what is happening in the story as you read it.

May lived in Spain.
One day it began to rain.
May baked a cake.
The cake looked like a snail.

She sailed on the lake.
She gave the cake to a friend.
Her friend's name was Cane.

Cane lived in a cave.
He was very brave.
Cane and May ate the snail cake.

Read the story once more. Read the questions below. Fill in the bubble by the correct answer.

1. Was it a rainy day? no ◯ yes ◯

2. Did May make a cage? no ◯ yes ◯

3. Did May sail to a cave? no ◯ yes ◯

4. How do you think Cane felt when May gave him the cake?

Write a title for the story.

Tell a friend what might happen next in the story.

Language arts application; reading and answering comprehension questions with long *a* word chunks.

www.summerbridgeactivities.com

Ii

Say each picture name. Listen for the **long _i_** sound \ī\ as in _slide_. Color the picture if its name has the long _i_ sound.

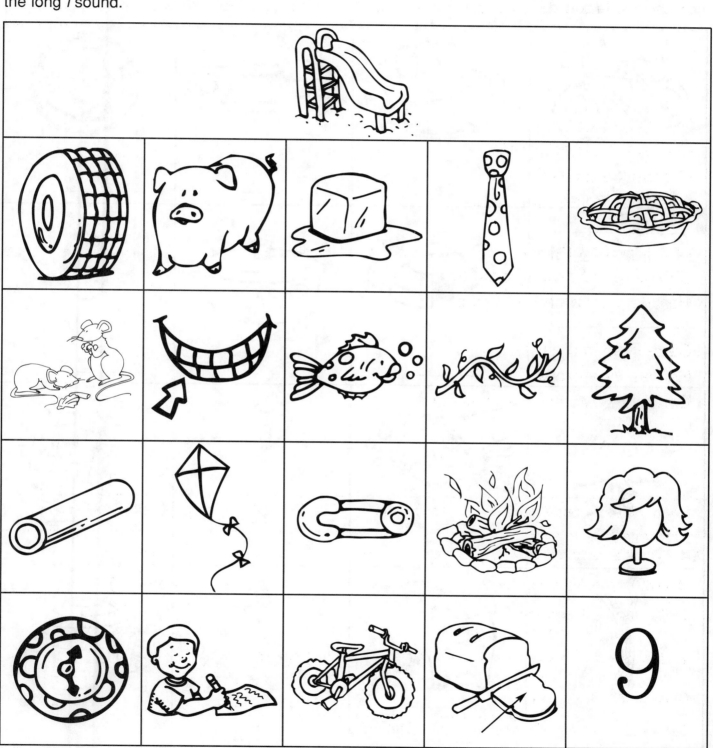

Introducing the long _i_ sound \ī\.

Name

Ii

Say each picture name. Listen for the *i* vowel sound. Print Ī if you hear the long *i* sound or Ĭ if you hear the short *i* sound.

Ĭ	ĭ	___	___
___	___	___	___
___	___	___	___
___	___	___	___

Using the sound of long *i* and short *i*.

Phonics Connection—Grade 1—RBP0237   www.summerbridgeactivities.com   ©RBP Books

Ii

kī te

Say each picture name. Listen for the *i* vowel sound. Print the word for the picture name.
Rule: If a word has two vowels, and one is final *e*, the first vowel is long and the *e* is silent.

dim · dime	pin · pine	fir · fire	bit · bite
dime			
fin · find	fill · file	rid · ride	kit · kite
pill · pile	till · tile	rip · ripe	sit · site
Tim · time	hill · hide	tip · tide	limb · line

Using the sound of long *i* and short *i*; word chunks with _*i*_e.

Ii

vīne sĭx

Say each picture name. Listen for the vowel sound. Print ī _e when you hear the long *i* sound. Print ĭ when you hear the short *i* sound.

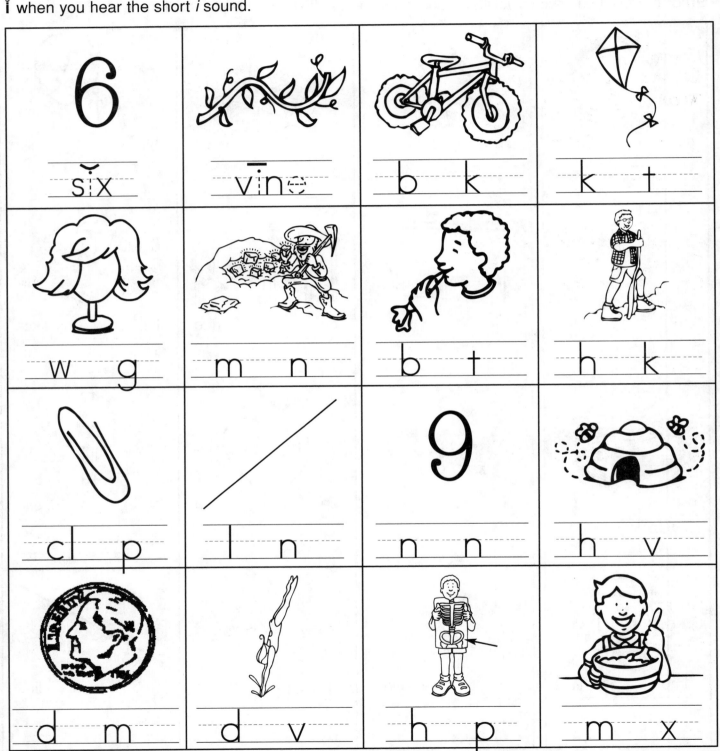

6 s<u>ĭ</u>x	 v<u>ī</u>ne	 b __ k	 k __ t
  w __ g	 m __ n	 b __ t	 h __ k
  c __ p	 __ n	9 n __ n	 h __ v
  d __ m	 d __ v	 h __ p	 m __ x

Using the sound of *i* review.

Phonics Connection—Grade 1—RBP0237   www.summerbridgeactivities.com   ©RBP Books

Ii

Say each picture name. Listen for the vowel sound. Fill in the bubble for the correct word. Print the word for the picture name.

○ pan ○ pane ● pine	○ kite ○ kit ○ Kate	○ tip ○ time ○ tire	○ fine ○ fill ○ file
pine			
○ time ○ tame ○ tin	○ dive ○ dime ○ dim	○ lip ○ lake ○ line	○ bike ○ bite ○ bat
○ hide ○ hive ○ hit	○ bike ○ bag ○ bake	○ mane ○ man ○ mine	○ dine ○ die ○ dive
○ ham ○ hill ○ hike	○ mitt ○ mix ○ mice	○ strip ○ stick ○ stripe	○ slide ○ Sid ○ slice

Using the sound of long *i* word chunks; standardized testing form.

www.summerbridgeactivities.com Phonics Connection—Grade 1—RBP0237

Name

Ii

Read each sentence. Read the three words. Look at the picture. Fill in the bubble next to the word that makes sense in the sentence. Print the word on the line.

1. The ~~kite~~ can fly high.	● kite ○ kit ○ Kate	
2. I can _____ .	○ dive ○ dim ○ date	
3. Kate likes to _____ .	○ hide ○ hate ○ hat	
4. Teddy had two _____ for pets.	○ met ○ make ○ mice	
5. We had a piece of _____ .	○ pie ○ pet ○ pat	
6. The bees flew in their _____ .	○ hive ○ high ○ have	

Using language arts; using context clues to select missing words with long *i* word chunks.

Phonics Connection—Grade 1—RBP0237   www.summerbridgeactivities.com   ©RBP Books

Name

Ii

Read the story below. Say each word. Listen carefully for the **long _i_** sound /ī/. Draw a line under each word with the long _i_ sound. Draw pictures of what is happening in the story as you read it.

<u>Mike</u> <u>likes</u> to <u>ride</u> his <u>bike</u>.
Six mice like to hide on the
bike with Mike.
Mike can bike for a mile.
He likes to go up to the top of
the hills.
He can go high into the pines.

Mike's bike gets a flat tire.
He has to take time to fix it.
It starts to rain.
The mice help him fix the tire.

Read the story once more. Read the questions below. Fill in the bubble by the correct answer.

1. Do five mice like to go with Mike? no ◯ yes ◯

2. Does Mike like to bike? no ◯ yes ◯

3. Will Mike ride high into the pines? no ◯ yes ◯

4. Who likes to ride the bike besides Mike? _____

Write a title for the story. _____

Tell a friend what might happen next in the story.

Language arts application; reading and answering comprehension questions with long _i_ word chunks.

Uu

Say each picture name. Listen for the **long *u*** sound \ū\ as in *ruler*. Color the picture if its name has the long *u* sound.

Introducing the long *u* sound \ū\.

www.summerbridgeactivities.com

Uu

Say each picture name. Listen for the **u** vowel sound. Print **ū** if you hear the long *u* sound or **ŭ** if you hear the short *u* sound.

Using the sound of long *u* and short *u*.

www.summerbridgeactivities.com   **Phonics Connection—Grade 1—RBP0237**

Name _____

Uu   tūbe̸

Say each picture name. Listen for the **u** vowel sound. Print the word for the picture name.
Rule: If a word has two vowels, and one is final *e*, the first vowel is long and the *e* is silent.

cub cube	tub tube	mull mule	rude rule
c u b e	_____	_____	_____
tuck tune	junk June	full flute	fuss fuse
_____	_____	_____	_____
dump dune	hug huge	us use	cut cute
_____	_____	_____	_____
buff bugle	fun fuel	rut ruler	cuff chute
_____	_____	_____	_____

Using the sound of long *u* and short *u* word chunks.

Phonics Connection—Grade 1—RBP0237   www.summerbridgeactivities.com   © RBP Books

Name

Uu

Say each picture name. Listen for the vowel sound. Print **_u _e** when you hear the long *u* sound.
Print **u** when you hear the short *u* sound.

c u b e   J __ n __   h __ g __   r __ __

m __ l __   d __ d __   t __ n __   d __ n __

c __ t __   f __ s __   fl __ t __   ch __ t __

pr __ n __   t __ b __   gl __ __   b l __ __

Using the sound of *u* review.

© RBP Books   www.summerbridgeactivities.com   Phonics Connection—Grade 1—RBP0237

Name

Uu

Say each picture name. Listen for the vowel sound. Fill in the bubble for the correct word. Print the word for the picture name.

○ cab ● cube ○ cub	○ tub ○ tube ○ tape	○ mutt ○ mud ○ mule	○ fun ○ fish ○ fuse
cube	_____	_____	_____
○ hug ○ huge ○ hat	○ din ○ dine ○ dune	○ cute ○ can ○ cut	○ dude ○ due ○ duke
_____	_____	_____	_____
○ rad ○ June ○ rug	○ rat ○ rug ○ rule	○ tune ○ hug ○ hut	○ mite ○ mule ○ flute
_____	_____	_____	_____

Using the sound of long *u* word chunks; standardizing testing form.

www.summerbridgeactivities.com ©RBP Books

Uu

Read each sentence. Read the three words. Look at the picture. Fill in the bubble next to the word that makes sense in the sentence. Print the word on the line.

1. June can play a ___tune___ .

- ● tune
- ○ tan
- ○ time

2. Kim fed the _____ .

- ○ mull
- ○ mule
- ○ mute

3. Hans had a _____ cake.

- ○ home
- ○ hug
- ○ huge

4. Put an ice _____ in the glass.

- ○ cube
- ○ cub
- ○ cake

5. Jan can blow a _____ .

- ○ bugle
- ○ bun
- ○ bin

6. We can ride on the lake in a _____ .

- ○ tube
- ○ tub
- ○ tab

Using language arts; using context clues to select missing words with *u* word chunks.

Uu

Read the story below. Say each word. Listen carefully for the **long _u_** sound \ū\. Draw a line under each word with the long _u_ sound. Draw pictures of what is happening in the story as you read it.

One hot day in June,

Kyle went for a ride on his mule.

The mule's name was Blue.

Blue and Kyle rode to the sand dunes.

As they rode along, Kyle played the flute.

Blue tried to sing a tune.

They stopped to get a huge glass of water with ice cubes in it.

They ate a prune.

Soon the sun was really hot.

They did not know what to do.

Read the story once more. Read the questions be_____ _____ _____bble by the correct answer.

1. Did Kyle ride a mule?   no ◯   yes ◯

2. Did Blue the mule play a flute?   no ◯   yes ◯

3. Where would you like to ride a mule? _____

_____

Write a title for the story. _____

_____

Tell a friend what might happen next in the story.

Language arts application; reading and answering comprehension questions with the long _u_ sound.

Oo

Say each picture name. Listen for the **long *o*** sound \ō\ as in *rope*. Color the picture if its name has the long *o* sound.

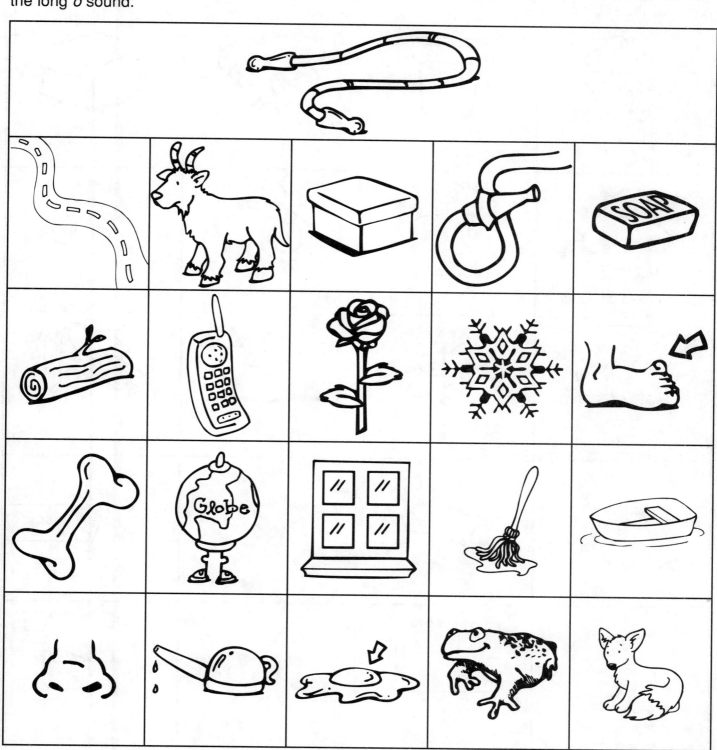

Introducing the long o sound \ō\.

www.summerbridgeactivities.com   **Phonics Connection—Grade 1—RBP0237**

Oo

Say each picture name. Listen for the *o* vowel sound. Print ō if you hear the long *o* sound or ŏ if you hear the short *o* sound.

ō

ŏ

Oo

nōte̸

Say each picture name. Listen for the **o** vowel sound. Print the word for the picture name.
Rule: If a word has two vowels, and one is final *e*, the first vowel is long and the *e* is silent.

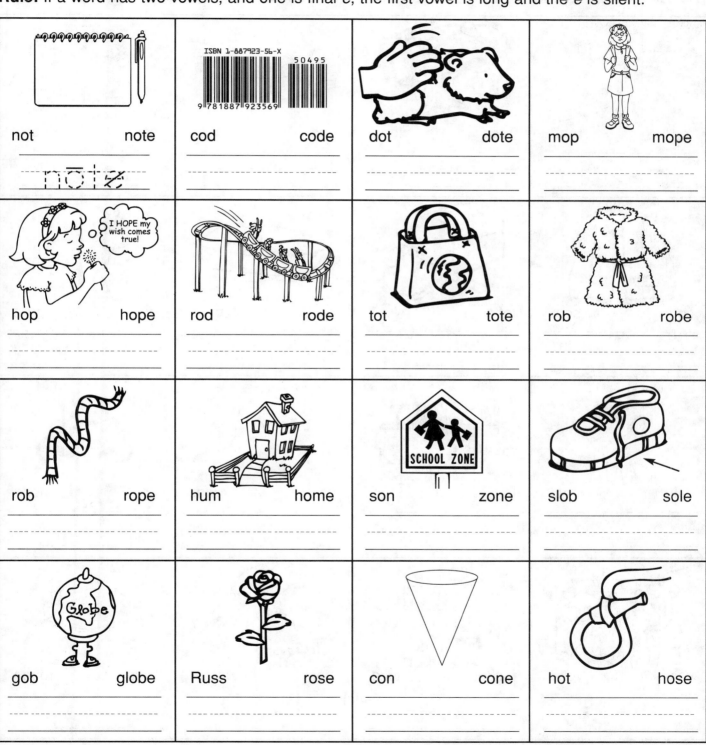

| not | note | cod | code | dot | dote | mop | mope |
| nōte̸ | | | | | | | |

| hop | hope | rod | rode | tot | tote | rob | robe |

| rob | rope | hum | home | son | zone | slob | sole |

| gob | globe | Russ | rose | con | cone | hot | hose |

Using the sound of long *o* and short *o*; _o_e.

© RBP Books

Oo

tōad

Say each picture name. Listen for the vowel sound. Print the word for the picture name.
Rule: In a word where two vowels are together, the first vowel usually is long and the second is silent.

rod	road	Todd	toad	nod	note	sow	soak
cot	coat	loft	loaf	bat	boat	got	goat
call	coal	lad	load	got	goal	not	nose
yak	yoke	jack	joke	clock	cloak	ranch	roach

Using the sound of long *o*; word chunks with *oa* and *_o_e*.

Name _____

Oo

rōad stōne tōe

Say each picture name. Listen for the vowel sound. Print **o_e** or **oa** when you hear the **long o** sound \ā\.

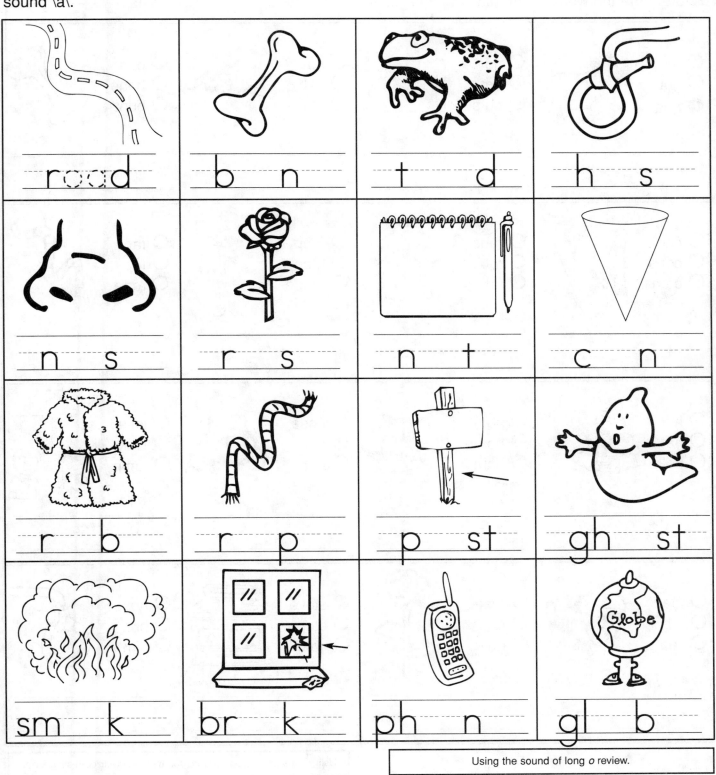

r o a d

b ___ ___ n

t ___ ___ d

h ___ ___ s

n ___ ___ s

r ___ ___ s

n ___ ___ t

c ___ ___ n

r ___ ___ b

r ___ ___ p

p ___ ___ st

gh ___ ___ st

sm ___ ___ k

br ___ ___ k

ph ___ ___ n

gl ___ ___ b

Using the sound of long *o* review.

www.summerbridgeactivities.com   **Phonics Connection—Grade 1—RBP0237**

Name

rōad stōne tōe

Say each picture name. Listen for the vowel sound. Fill in the bubble next to the word for the picture. Print the word for the picture name.

○ go ○ got ● goat	○ no ○ not ○ note	○ so ○ sob ○ stone	○ bun ○ bone ○ bunt
goat			
○ can ○ cone ○ came	○ robe ○ rob ○ rat	○ mop ○ map ○ mope	○ rad ○ rap ○ rope
○ hut ○ hat ○ hole	○ hum ○ home ○ ham	○ nose ○ note ○ not	○ joke ○ jack ○ jump Knock, knock! Who's there?
○ toad ○ tub ○ Ted	○ rose ○ run ○ rib	○ stove ○ stop ○ soak	○ hose ○ hot ○ him

Using the sound of long *o* word chunks; standardized testing form.

Oo

Read each sentence. Read the three words. Look at the picture. Fill in the bubble next to the word that makes sense in the sentence. Print the word on the line.

1. The boat has a ___pole___ .	○ pat ○ pin ● pole	
2. He gave a _____ to his mom.	○ bone ○ rose ○ rat	
3. John wrote a _____ to Joan.	○ nose ○ note ○ not	
4. The _____ is on the road.	○ tub ○ toad ○ tot	
5. The mole dug a _____	○ hat ○ hot ○ hole	
6. Ty tells us a _____	○ joke ○ jack ○ jump	Knock, knock! Who's there?

Using language arts; using context clues to select words with long *o* word chunks.

www.summerbridgeactivities.com   Phonics Connection—Grade 1—RBP0237

Oo

Read the story below. Say each word. Listen carefully for the **long *o*** sound. Draw a line under each word with the long *o* sound. Draw pictures of what is happening in the story as you read it.

In October a <u>toad</u>

tried to cross the road.

On her way

she got delayed.

She wrote a note

to her friend the goat

She put out her nose

to smell the rose.

She took off her cloak

to take a soak.

She ate a cone

on top of the dog bone.

She saw a doe

and stubbed her toe.

Read the story once more. Read the questions below. Fill in the bubble by the correct answer.

1. Did the toad try to cross the road in September?   no ◯ yes ◯

2. Did she smell a rose?   no ◯ yes ◯

3. Do you think she ever crossed the road? _____

_____

Write a title for the story. _____

_____

Tell a friend what might happen next in the story.

Language arts application; reading and answering comprehension questions with the long *o* sound.

Ee

Say each picture name. Listen for the **long *e*** sound \ē\ as in *needle*. Color the picture if its name has the long *e* sound.

Introducing the long *e* sound \ē\.

Ee

jēep jĕt

Say each picture name. Listen for the *e* vowel sound. Print **ē** if you hear the long *e* sound or **ĕ** if you hear the short *e* sound.

Using the sound of long *e* and short *e*.

Phonics Connection—Grade 1—RBP0237
www.summerbridgeactivities.com
©**RBP Books**

Name _____

Ee

sēal

Say each picture name. Listen for the **e** vowel sound. Print the word for the picture name.
Rule: In a word where two vowels are together, the first vowel usually is long, and the second is silent.

met meat	bed bead	sale seal	set seat
mēat			
net neat	red read	melt meal	pass peas
Ben bean	pea peach	bed beach	led leaf
beck beak	men mean	shed seat	Jen jeans

Using the sound of long *e*; word chunks *ea*.

www.summerbridgeactivities.com
Phonics Connection—Grade 1—RBP0237

Name

Ee

jēep

Say each picture name. Listen for the vowel sound. Print the word for the picture name.
Rule: In a word where two vowels are together, the first vowel usually is long, and the second is silent.

jet jeep	wed weed	pep peep	bed bee
fed feed	bell beep	wet weep	ten teen
fell feel	bet beet	set seed	Kent knee
tent tree	hem heel	bet beef	pet peel

Using the sound of long *e*; word chunk *ee*.

www.summerbridgeactivities.com

Ee

Say each picture name. Listen for the vowel sound. Print **ea** or **ee** when you hear the **long e** sound.

f _ _ t   b _ _ t   s _ _ t   j _ _ p

p _ _ k   b _ _ d   b _ _ p   b _ _ k

b _ _ n   r _ _ d   p _ _ s   m _ _ l

w _ _ d   s _ _ d   tr _ _   b _ _

Using the sound of long *ee* and *ea* word chunks.

© RBP Books   www.summerbridgeactivities.com   **Phonics Connection—Grade 1—RBP0237**

Name

Ee

jēep sēat

Say each picture name. Listen for the vowel sound. Fill in the bubble next to the word for the picture. Print the word for the picture name.

○ feet ● feel ○ feed	○ met ○ mean ○ meat	○ heel ○ hole ○ have	○ sale ○ seal ○ sea
feel			
○ peel ○ peas ○ pole	○ feet ○ fed ○ feel	○ lead ○ load ○ leaf	○ bell ○ bee ○ bean
○ bed ○ bead ○ beck	○ time ○ tame ○ team	○ jeep ○ deep ○ creep	○ beef ○ beet ○ bet
○ beach ○ bead ○ beat	○ peach ○ pea ○ peek	○ mean ○ met ○ men	○ beak ○ bee ○ beam

Using the sound of long *e*; standardized testing form.

Phonics Connection—Grade 1—RBP0237   www.summerbridgeactivities.com   ©RBP Books

Name

Ee

jēep sēat

Read each sentence. Read the three words. Look at the picture. Fill in the bubble next to the word that makes sense in the sentence. Print the word on the line.

1. I have a green ⟨leaf⟩ .

○ bean
○ gate
● leaf

2. The big _____ was turning.

○ wheel
○ wet
○ weed

3. The peach was _____ .

○ set
○ sweet
○ sun

4. I saw a _____ on the road.

○ sleep
○ shut
○ sheep

5. We rode in a blue _____ .

○ jump
○ jeep
○ jam

6. We have a good _____ .

○ team
○ tam
○ tune

Using language arts; using context clues to select missing words with long *e* word chunks.

© RBP Books   www.summerbridgeactivities.com   Phonics Connection—Grade 1—RBP0237

Ee

Read the story below. Say each word. Listen carefully for the long *e* sound. Draw a line under each word with the **long e** sound. Draw pictures of what is happening in the story as you read it.

Jean went to the beach.

She rode in a green jeep.

She walked down to the shore.

She sat in the sand.

She took time to read a book.

She went for a walk and saw a bee.

She picked up a bead, a shell, and a seed.

She stopped to eat a beet and a peach under the tree.

Then she could not find her green jeep.

Read the story once more. Read the questions below. Fill in the bubble by the correct answer.

1. Did Jean go to the forest?   no ◯   yes ◯

2. Did she read a book?   no ◯   yes ◯

3. Did she ride in her green jeep?   no ◯   yes ◯

4. Do you think she liked the beach? _____

Write a title for the story. _____

Tell a friend what might happen next in the story.

Language arts application; reading and answering comprehension questions with long *e* word chunks.

Yy

fly(ī) baby(ē)

Read the words and look at the pictures. Fill in the circle next to the sound **y** makes in each word.
Rule: The letter *y* at the end of some words can stand for the long *i* sound, as in *fly*. The letter *y* at the end of some words can also stand for the long *e* sound, as in *baby*.

○ *y* ● long *i* ○ long *e* cry	○ *y* ○ long *i* ○ long *e* puppy	○ *y* ○ long *i* ○ long *e* yam
○ *y* ○ long *i* ○ long *e* pony	○ *y* ○ long *i* ○ long *e* yell	○ *y* ○ long *i* ○ long *e* fly
○ *y* ○ long *i* ○ long *e* yak	○ *y* ○ long *i* ○ long *e* windy	○ *y* ○ long *i* ○ long *e* sky
○ *y* ○ long *i* ○ long *e* baby	○ *y* ○ long *i* ○ long *e* spy	○ *y* ○ long *i* ○ long *e* yard

> Sounds of *y* as in *yak*, *y* as in *fry*, and *y* as in *story*.

www.summerbridgeactivities.com Phonics Connection—Grade 1—RBP0237

Name

Yy

fly(ī) baby(ē)

Look at the picture in each box. Look at the word under the picture. Read the words at the side of the picture. Fill in the bubble next to the word that has the same sound as the picture.

Rule: The letter *y* at the end of some words can stand for the long *i* sound, as in *fry*. The letter *y* at the end of some words can also stand for the long *e* sound, as in *story*.

● baby ○ fly ○ yam penny	○ sky ○ sunny ○ yell lady	○ yes ○ shy ○ Sally yam
○ dolly ○ sly ○ kitty fry	○ why ○ silly ○ yellow happy	○ jelly ○ my ○ your tummy
○ sky ○ many ○ yet daddy	**60** ○ by ○ busy ○ why sixty	○ carry ○ pretty ○ my sky
○ fly ○ hobby ○ yam city	○ every ○ try ○ yoke baby	○ yep ○ puppy ○ young lazy

Sounds of *y* as in *yak*, *y* as in *fry*, and *y* as in *story*.

www.summerbridgeactivities.com   ©RBP Books

Name

Yy

fly(ī) baby(ē)

Read each sentence. Read the three words. Look at the picture. Fill in the bubble next to the word that makes sense in the sentence. Print the word on the line.

Rule: The letter *y* at the end of some words can stand for the long *i* sound, as in *fry*. The letter *y* at the end of some words can also stand for the long *e* sound, as in *story*.

1. We went to the farm every _year._	● year ○ very ○ sly	
2. The _____ days were warm.	○ muddy ○ sunny ○ yak	
3. We were very _____.	○ happy ○ yellow ○ why	
4. We saw a puppy and a _____.	○ yes ○ try ○ pony	
5. The lady read us a _____.	○ story ○ fly ○ hobby	
6. A _____ landed on my food.	○ lady ○ daddy ○ fly	
7. We went back to the _____.	○ city ○ yak ○ why	

Using language arts; using context clues to select missing *y* words.

www.summerbridgeactivities.com   **Phonics Connection—Grade 1—RBP0237**

-ed, -ing

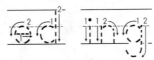

Look at the pictures. Read each word. Write the base word.

Rule: A word to which an ending can be added is called a **base word.** The base word of *fished* is *fish*. The base word of *fishing* is *fish*.

fishing ──── fish	mailed ────────	played ────────
singing ────────	jumped ────────	raining ────────
floating ────────	filled ────────	passing ────────
nailed ────────	brushing ────────	mashed ────────

Introducing base words with *-ed* and *-ing* endings.

Name

-ed, -ing

Look at the pictures. Read each base word. Add the ending to the base word.

Rule: A word to which an ending can be added is called a **base word.** The base word of *fished* is *fish*. The base word of *fishing* is *fish*.

		Add **-ed**		Add **-ing**
fish		*fished*		*fishing*
toss				
fill				
box				
dress				
float				
sail				
help				

Using base words with *-ed* and *-ing* endings.

www.summerbridgeactivities.com
Phonics Connection—Grade 1—RBP0237

Name

-ed, -ing

Look at the pictures. Read each sentence. Fill in the bubble for the correct word to finish the sentence. Write the word on the line. Reread the story after you have filled in the words.

1. We went to the lake to __fish__.	● fish ○ fished ○ fishing	
2. Lori _____ by the shore of the lake.	○ play ○ played ○ playing	
3. I _____ for a fish to bite my worm.	○ wait ○ waited ○ waiting	
4. Mom was _____ us some food to eat.	○ make ○ made ○ making	
5. We _____ to get cold.	○ start ○ started ○ starting	
6. We _____ we had our coats.	○ wish ○ wished ○ wishing	

Using language art; using context clues to select missing words with *-ed* and *-ing* endings.

Name

-s, -es

Look at the pictures. Read the words below. Add **-s** or **-es** to each word to make it mean "more than one."

Rule: You can make some words mean "more than one" by adding *-s* to the base word. When a word ends in *s, sh, ch, x,* or *z,* add *-es* to the base word to make it mean "more than one."

Examples: dogs   axes   buses   dishes   lunches   dresses

boat		_boats_
can		
glass		
hat		
mix		
brush		
peach		
tree		

Introducing base words with *-s* or *-es* added to form plurals.

143

© RBP Books   www.summerbridgeactivities.com   Phonics Connection—Grade 1—RBP0237

-s, -es

Look at the pictures. Read the words below. Circle the base word.

Rule: You can make some words mean "more than one" by adding -s to the base word. When a word ends in s, sh, ch, x, or z, add -es to the base word to make it mean "more than one."

Examples: dogs axes buses dishes lunches dresses

apples	bags	crabs	cans	desks
dogs	faces	mops	trees	radios
buses	boxes	dishes	foxes	kisses
patches	peaches	boys	days	keys
plays	says	valleys	whales	toads

Using base words with -s or -es added to nouns to form plurals.

Name

-s, -es

Look at the pictures. Read the words below. Fill in the circle for the correct word. Fill in the sentence.
Rule: You can make some words mean "more than one" by adding -s to the base word. When a word ends in *s, sh, ch, x,* or *z,* add *-es* to the base word to make it mean "more than one."
Examples: dog*s*   ax*es*   bus*es*   dish*es*   lunch*es*   dress*es*

The _boys_ wanted to play a game.	● boys ○ clams ○ toads	
They went out to the peach _____.	○ quizzes ○ beds ○ trees	
They took some _____ with them.	○ mops ○ cans ○ buses	
Hitting cans with _____ was fun.	○ peaches ○ kisses ○ valleys	
The _____ would chase the peaches.	○ dogs ○ days ○ radios	
The boys ate _____ and went home.	○ clams ○ apples ○ lunches	

Read the story once more. Read the questions below. Fill in the bubble by the correct answer.

1. Did the boys go to the forest?   no ○   yes ○

2. Did they take peaches with them?   no ○   yes ○

3. Do you think they like to play in the trees? _____

Why? _____

Write a title for the story. _____

Tell a friend what might happen next in the story.

Language arts application; reading and answering comprehension questions with *-s* or *-es* added to form plurals.

www.summerbridgeactivities.com   Phonics Connection—Grade 1—RBP0237

Contractions

Read the list of words below. Fill in the bubble for the contraction that means the same as the words.

A **contraction** is a short way to write two words. It is written by putting two words together and leaving out a letter or letters. An **apostrophe** (') takes the place of the letter or letters that are left out.

Example: can   not   drop the letters *n* and *o* from *not* to make the word **can't**

can not	**I am**	**have not**	**would not**
○ couldn't ○ could've ● can't	○ I'd ○ I'll ○ I'm	○ hasn't ○ haven't ○ hadn't	○ wouldn't ○ we're ○ what's
could not	**I will**	**has not**	**what is**
○ couldn't ○ could've ○ can't	○ I'd ○ I'll ○ I'm	○ hasn't ○ haven't ○ hadn't	○ we'll ○ we're ○ what's
could have	**I have**	**they are**	**we had**
○ couldn't ○ could've ○ can't	○ I'd ○ I've ○ I'm	○ they're ○ that'll ○ there's	○ we'll ○ we'd ○ what's
do not	**it is**	**had not**	**who will**
○ didn't ○ don't ○ doesn't	○ it's ○ I'll ○ I'm	○ hasn't ○ haven't ○ hadn't	○ who'll ○ we're ○ what's
we are	**she is**	**you had**	**we will**
○ we've ○ wouldn't ○ we're	○ she'd ○ she's ○ shouldn't	○ you'd ○ you've ○ you're	○ we'll ○ we're ○ what's

Introducing contractions.

www.summerbridgeactivities.com

Contractions

Read each contraction below. Then write the two words for which each contraction stands.

A **contraction** is a short way to write two words. It is written by putting two words together and leaving out a letter or letters. An **apostrophe** (') takes the place of the letter or letters that are left out.

Example: **you** **are** drop the letter *a* from *are* to make the word **you're**

you're	you	are
she'd		
they've		
that's		
didn't		
let's		
he'll		
isn't		

Using contractions.

www.summerbridgeactivities.com **Phonics Connection—Grade 1—RBP0237**

Contractions

Read the story below. Write the contraction for which each set of two words stands.

    A **contraction** is a short way to write two words. It is written by putting two words together and leaving out a letter or letters. An **apostrophe** (') takes the place of the letter or letters that are left out.

Example: can   **not**   drop the letters *n* and *o* from *not* to make the word **can't**

We're _____ going to Grandmother's house. _____ be glad to see us.

We are   **She will**

We _____ surprise her. _____ play ball with my cousin Sam.

should not   **I will**

_____ go riding the horses. _____ fun riding in the hills.

We will   **It is**

Grandmother _____ cook. _____ a pizza lover and will order pizza for us.

does not   **She is**

Read the story once more. Read the questions below. Fill in the space by the correct answer.

1. Were they going to Grandma's house?   no ◯   yes ◯

2. Would they ride donkeys?   no ◯   yes ◯

3. Do you think it would be fun to ride in the hills on horses? _____

    Why? _____

_____

Write a title for the story. _____

Tell a friend what might happen next in the story.

Using contractions in context.

Name

Compound Words

A **compound word** is a word made up of two smaller words. Look at the pictures. Write the two small words for the top pictures. Then write the compound word under the bottom picture.

boat   sail

sailboat

Introducing compound words.

149

Name

Compound words

A **compound word** is a word made up of two smaller words. Look at the pictures. Write the two small words for the top pictures. Then write the compound word under the bottom picture.

Phonics Connection—Grade 1—RBP0237   www.summerbridgeactivities.com   © RBP Books

Name

ABC Order

Put the letters in the correct order.
a b c d e f g h i j k l m n o p q r s t u v w x y z

D A C B	H E F G	I K J L	N M P O
ABCD			
R Q S T	V U X W	Y Z B A	C E D F
d a c b	h e f g	i k l j	m n p o
t s q r	v x w u	z y b a	d f c e

Alphabetical order.

www.summerbridgeactivities.com Phonics Connection—Grade 1—RBP0237

Name

ABC Order

Write **Yes** if the words are in ABC order.
Write **No** if the words are not in ABC order.

cat fat mat _____ yes	hat bat pat _____ no	can man ran _____	nap tap zap _____
ram Sam ham _____	dad bad had _____	ax Max wax _____	tag sag shag _____
fit kit Sid _____	fin pin win _____	dip hip trip _____	big pig wig _____
fix six mix _____	run fun sun _____	cut nut but _____	cub rub sub _____
pot got cot _____	mop pop top _____	dog frog hog _____	cob mob job _____
jet bet wet _____	pen men ten _____	beg leg peg _____	best vest pest _____

Alphabetical order.

Phonics Connection—Grade 1—RBP0237 www.summerbridgeactivities.com

Name

High Frequency Word List

Cut out the cards and practice saying the words.

a	about
again	any
are	because
been	could

High frequency words.

© RBP Books   www.summerbridgeactivities.com   Phonics Connection—Grade 1—RBP0237

High Frequency Word List

Cut out the cards and practice saying the words.

do	does
down	each
have	know
little	many

High frequency words.

(154)

© RBP Books

High Frequency Word List

Cut out the cards and practice saying the words.

more	most
of	one
only	other
people	said

High frequency words.

www.summerbridgeactivities.com Phonics Connection—Grade 1—RBP0237

High Frequency Word List

Cut out the cards and practice saying the words.

some	than
the	their
there	these
they	this

High frequency words.

High Frequency Word List

Cut out the cards and practice saying the words.

through	to
two	use
very	was
were	what

High frequency words.

www.summerbridgeactivities.com

Phonics Connection—Grade 1—RBP0237

High Frequency Word List

Cut out the cards and practice saying the words.

where	which
who	with
words	would
you	your

High frequency words.

www.summerbridgeactivities.com

© RBP Books

Answer Pages

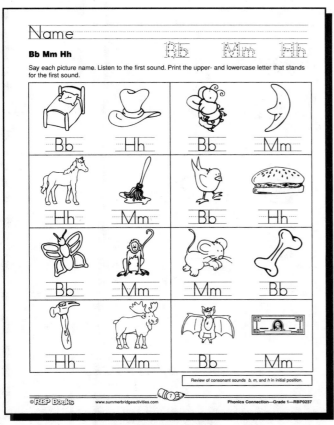

Page 7

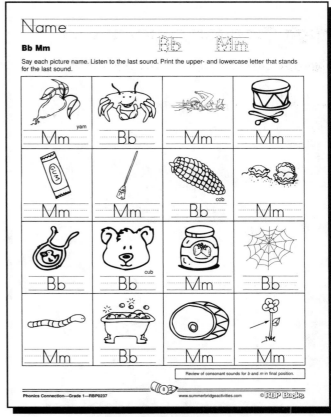

Page 8

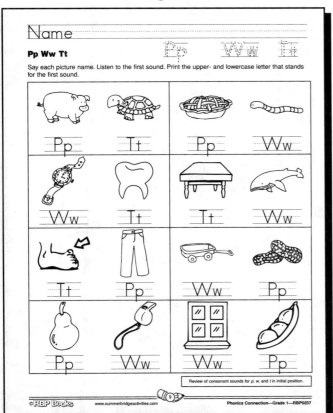

Page 9

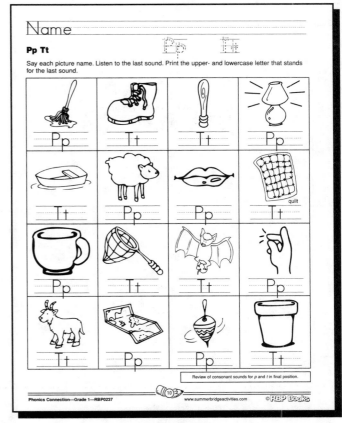

Page 10

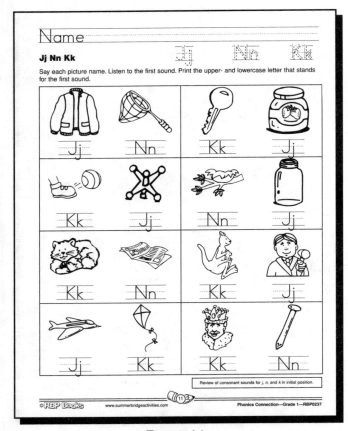

Page 11

Page 12

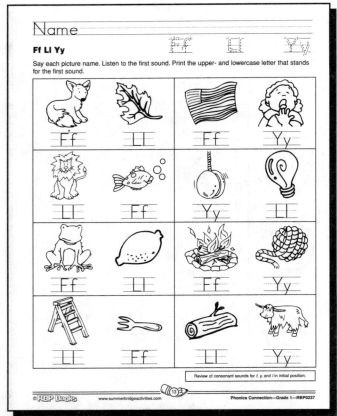

Page 13

Page 14

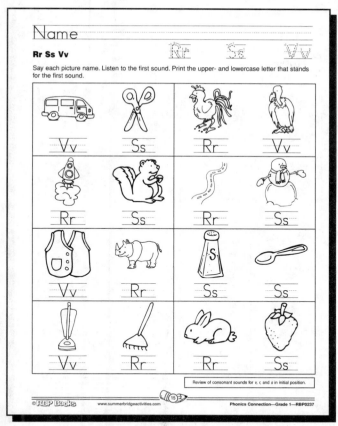

Page 15

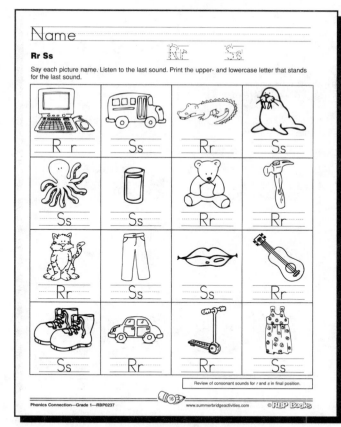

Page 16

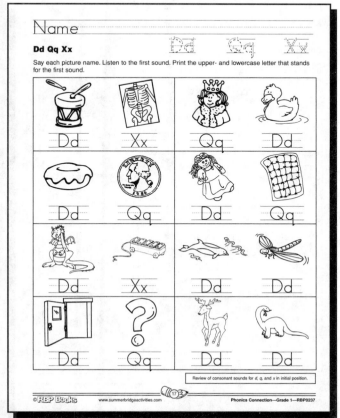

Page 17

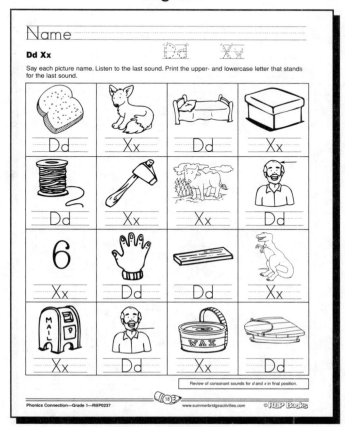

Page 18

www.summerbridgeactivities.com Phonics Connection—Grade 1—RBP0237

Answer Pages

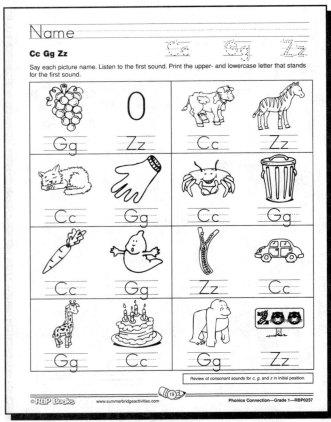

Page 19

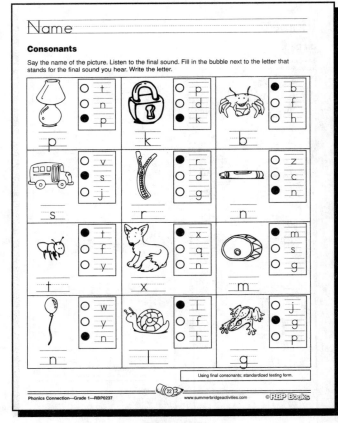

Page 20

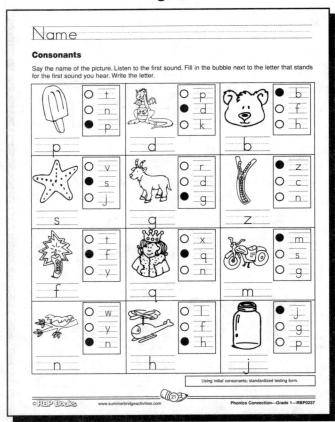

Page 21

Page 22

Answer Pages

Page 23

Name

Aa

Say each picture name. Listen for the **short** *a* sound \a\ as in *apple*. Color the picture if its name has the short a sound.

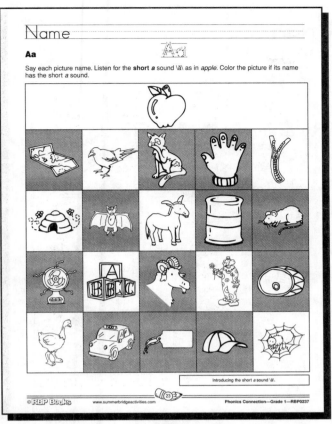

Introducing the short a sound \a\.

Page 23

Page 24

Name

Aa

Look at the letters in the rubber band. Stretch out the sounds; then snap them together to make the word. Say "b—" "a—" "t—" "bat." Print the word.

b a t   c a t

m a t   h a t

r a t   p a t

f a t   b a t

s a t   ch a t

Using the sound of short a; word chunk at.

Page 24

Page 25

Name

Aa

Look at the letters in the rubber band. Stretch out the sounds; then snap them together to make the word. Say "c—" "a—" "n—" "can." Print the word. Draw a line from the word to the picture.

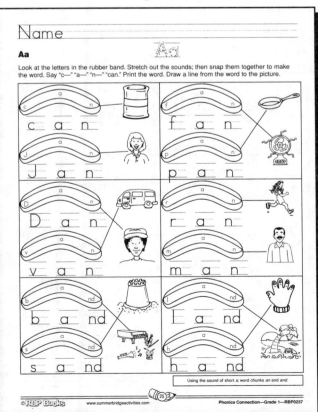

c a n   f a n

J a n   p a n

D a n   r a n

v a n   m a n

b a nd   l a nd

s a nd   h a nd

Using the sound of short a; word chunks an and and.

Page 25

Page 26

Name

Aa

Look at the letters in the rubber band. Stretch out the sounds; then snap them together to make the word. Say "c—" "a—" "p—" "cap." Add the beginning sound from the box to make a word. Print the word.

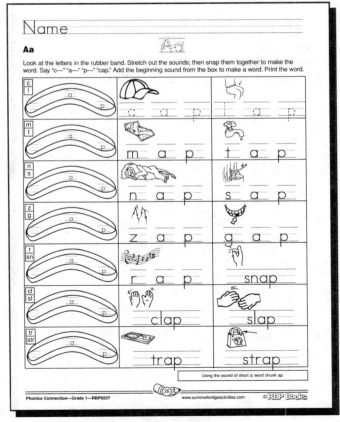

c a p   c a p

m a p   t a p

n a p   s a p

z a p   g a p

r a p   snap

clap   slap

trap   strap

Using the sound of short a; word chunk ap.

Page 26

Answer Pages

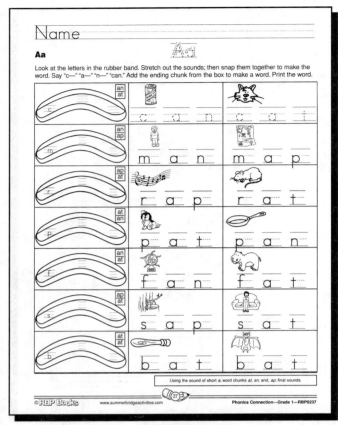

Page 27

Name

Aa

Look at the letters in the rubber band. Stretch out the sounds; then snap them together to make the word. Say "c—" "a—" "n—" "can." Add the ending chunk from the box to make a word. Print the word.

Say each picture name. Listen for the **short** *a* sound \ă\. Print *a* if you hear the short *a* sound.

ram   dam   jam   ham

clam   yam   bag   rag

wag   tag   zag   shag

flag   sag   dad   lad

pad   bad   mad   sad

Using the sound of short *a*; review of the middle short *a* word chunks *am, ag, ad*.

Page 28

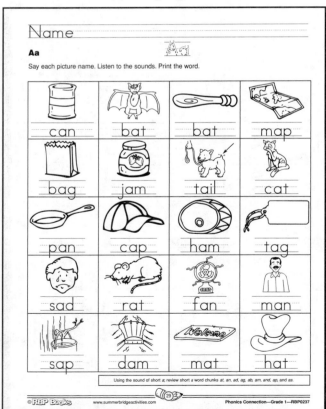

Page 29

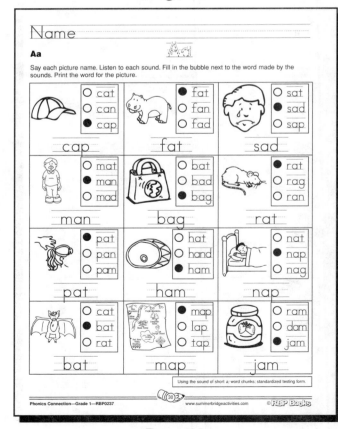

Page 30

Answer Pages

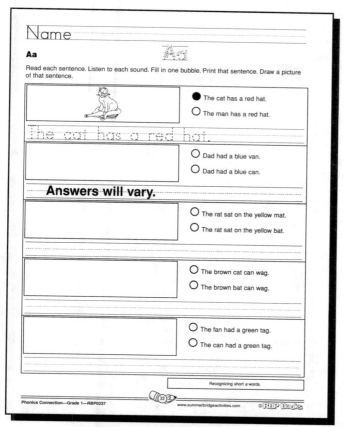

Name

Aa

Read each sentence. Listen to each sound. Fill in one bubble. Print that sentence. Draw a picture of that sentence.

1. ● The cat has a red hat.
   ○ The man has a red hat.

The cat has a red hat.

2. ○ Dad had a blue van.
   ○ Dad had a blue can.

Answers will vary.

3. ○ The rat sat on the yellow mat.
   ○ The rat sat on the yellow bat.

4. ○ The brown cat can wag.
   ○ The brown bat can wag.

5. ○ The fan had a green tag.
   ○ The can had a green tag.

Recognizing short *a* words.

Phonics Connection—Grade 1—RBP0237   www.summerbridgeactivities.com   ©RBP Books   32

Pages 32, 47, 62, 77, 92

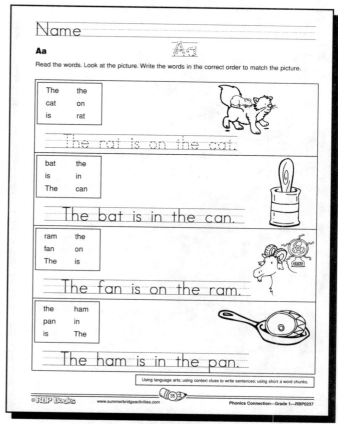

Name

Aa

Read each sentence. Print a word that rhymes with the underlined word. Make the sentence tell about the picture to the right.

1. The fat <u>cat</u> sat on a **bat**.
2. The man had a <u>tag</u> on a **bag**.
3. Pam is <u>sad</u> and **mad**.
4. <u>Max</u> had an **axe**.
5. Jan has a <u>pan</u> and a **can**.
6. The <u>cap</u> is on the **lap**.
7. Dad had a <u>nap</u> on the **map**.
8. Sam had <u>jam</u> and **ham**.

Using language arts; rhyming words; using context clues to select rhyming words with short *a* chunks.

©RBP Books   www.summerbridgeactivities.com   33   Phonics Connection—Grade 1—RBP0237

Page 33

Name

Aa

Read each sentence. Read the three words. Look at the picture. Fill in the bubble next to the word that makes sense in the sentence. Print the word on the line.

1. Dan has a **bat**.
   ● bat
   ○ wag
   ○ had

2. Max had a **ram**.
   ● ram
   ○ pat
   ○ sad

3. Dad has a **band**.
   ○ land
   ○ sand
   ● band

4. Ann sat on a **hat**.
   ○ cab
   ● hat
   ○ bad

5. The rat ran to the **lad**.
   ○ wax
   ○ rap
   ● lad

6. Zack had a **ham**.
   ● ham
   ○ sand
   ○ fad

Using language arts; using context clues to select missing words with short *a* chunks.

Phonics Connection—Grade 1—RBP0237   www.summerbridgeactivities.com   ©RBP Books   34

Page 34

Name

Aa

Read the words. Look at the picture. Write the words in the correct order to match the picture.

The	the
cat	on
is	rat

The rat is on the cat.

bat	the
is	in
The	can

The bat is in the can.

ram	the
fan	on
The	is

The fan is on the ram.

the	ham
pan	in
is	The

The ham is in the pan.

Using language arts; using context clues to write sentences; using short *a* word chunks.

©RBP Books   www.summerbridgeactivities.com   35   Phonics Connection—Grade 1—RBP0237

Page 35

Answer Pages

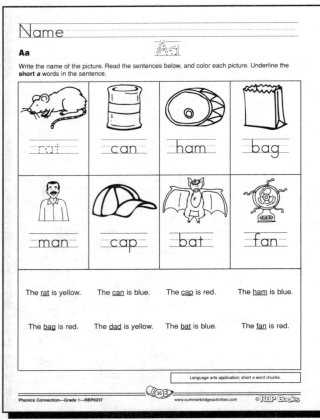

Page 36

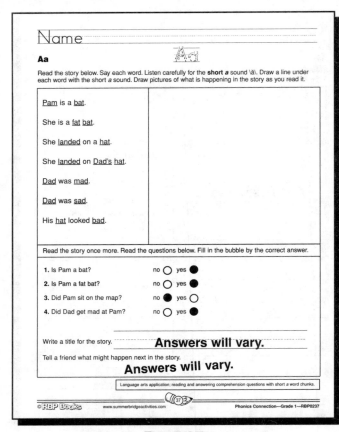

Page 37

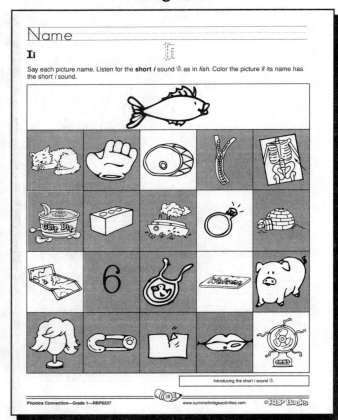

Page 38

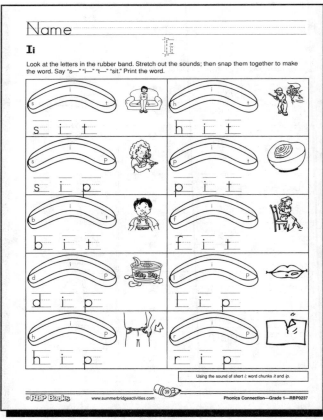

Page 39

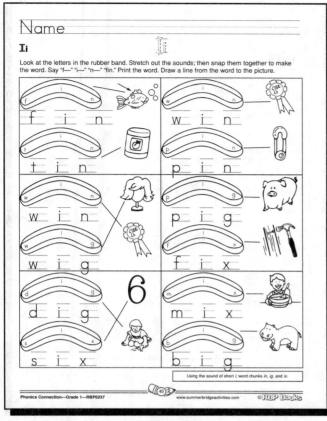

Page 40

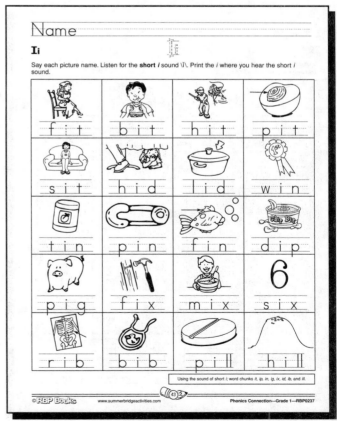

Page 41

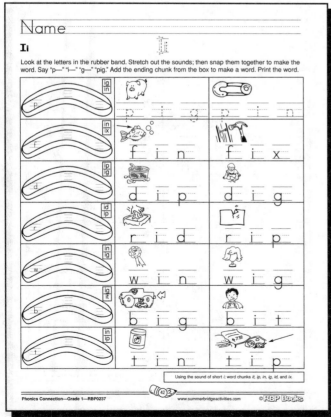

Page 42

Say each picture name. Listen for the **short i** sound \i\. Print the *i* where you hear the short *i* sound.

f i t   b i t   h i t   p i t

s i t   h i d   l i d   w i n

t i n   p i n   f i n   d i p

p i g   f i x   m i x   s i x

r i b   b i b   p i l l   h i l l

Page 43

www.summerbridgeactivities.com

Phonics Connection—Grade 1—RBP0237

Answer Pages

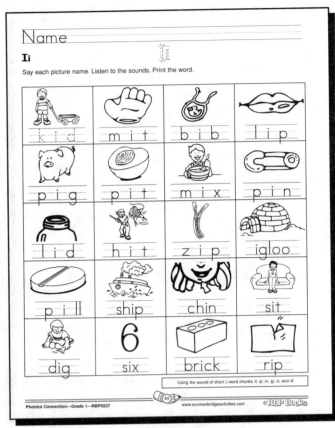

Page 44

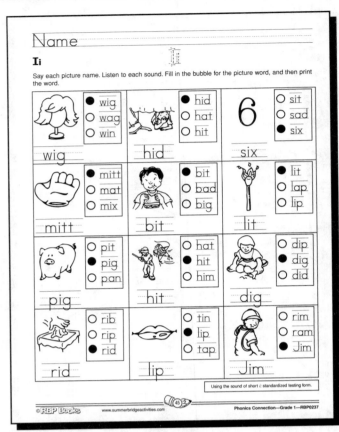

Page 45

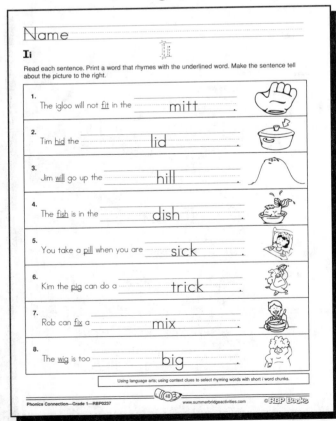

Page 48

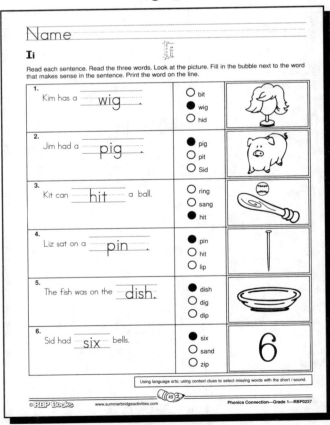

Page 49

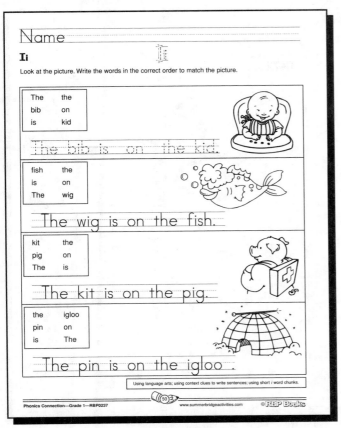

Page 50

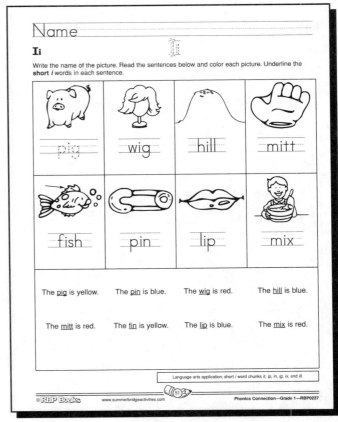

Page 51

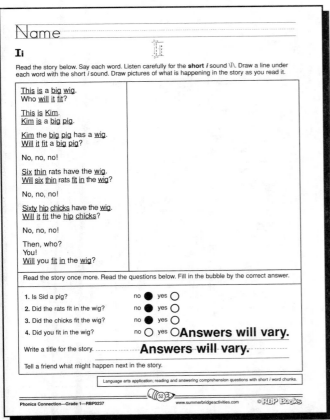

Page 52

Page 53

Answer Pages

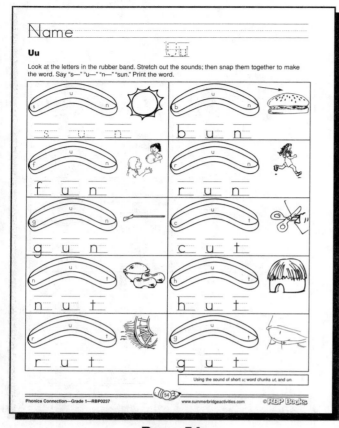

Page 54

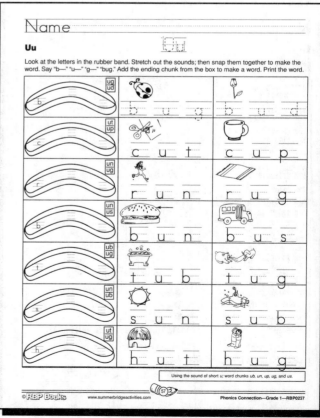

Page 55

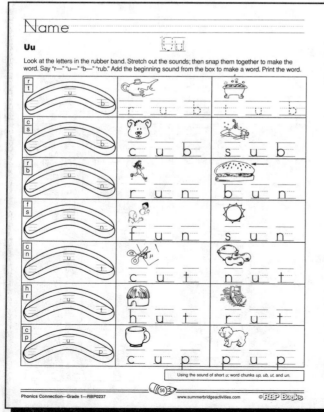

Page 56

Page 57

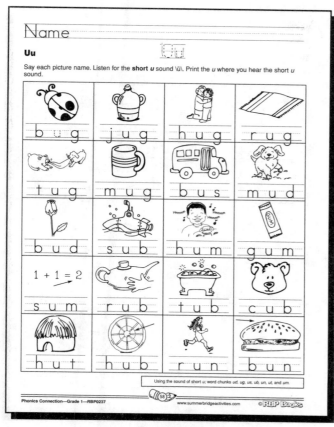

Page 58

Page 59

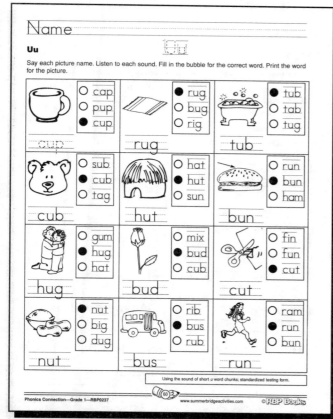

Page 60

Page 63

www.summerbridgeactivities.com

Phonics Connection—Grade 1—RBP0237

Answer Pages

Page 64

Name

Uu

Read each sentence. Read the three words. Look at the picture. Fill in the bubble next to the word that makes sense in the sentence. Print the word on the line.

1. Bud has a big cub .
   - ● cub
   - ○ cut
   - ○ cat

2. Russ had a nut .
   - ○ hut
   - ● nut
   - ○ hit

3. Gus can run to the bus .
   - ○ tub
   - ● bus
   - ○ sun

4. Jim ate a bun in the sun .
   - ● sun
   - ○ jug
   - ○ tub

5. The hut was on the mud .
   - ● mud
   - ○ sub
   - ○ gum

6. Tug can hum for us.
   - ● hum
   - ○ fun
   - ○ jug

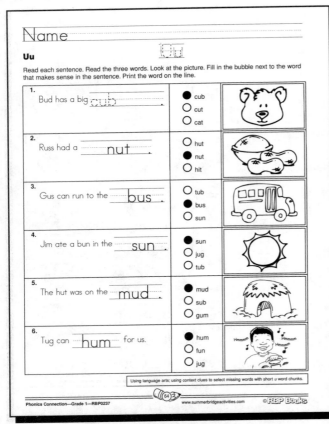

Using language arts; using context clues to select missing words with short u word chunks.

Page 65

Name

Uu

Read the words. Look at the picture. Write the words in the correct order to match the picture.

The	the
bug	on
is	tub

The bug is on the tub.

mud	the
is	on
The	rug

The mud is on the rug.

nut	the
mug	in
The	is

The nut is in the mug.

the	sub
cub	in
is	The

The cub is in the sub.

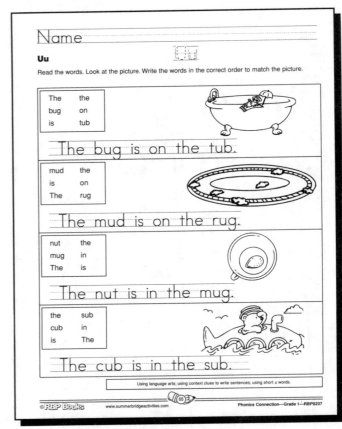

Using language arts; using context clues to write sentences; using short u words.

Page 66

Name

Uu

Write the name of the picture. Read the sentences below and color each picture. Underline the short *u* words in each sentence.

gum   sub   cup   pup

cub   nut   hut   sun

The cub is green.   The nut is purple.   The hut is red.   The sub is blue.

The pup is red.   The sun is yellow.   The cup is green.   The gum is blue.

Language arts application; short u word chunks up, ut, ub, un, and um.

Page 67

Name

Uu

Read the story below. Say each word. Listen carefully for the **short u** sound \ŭ\. Draw a line under each word with the short *u* sound. Draw pictures of what is happening in the story as you read it.

"Kim's pup is bad," said Bud to Gus.

"He tugs on rugs.

He bats at bugs.

He tips mugs.

He digs in the mud.

He is a bad pup.

He hid my gum!"

"He is not bad," said Gus.

"He is a fun pup, and fun pups dig and tug."

"This is not fun. I want my gum," said Bud.

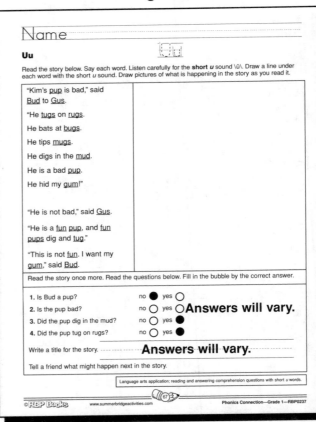

Read the story once more. Read the questions below. Fill in the bubble by the correct answer.

1. Is Bud a pup?   no ● yes ○
2. Is the pup bad?   no ○ yes ○ **Answers will vary.**
3. Did the pup dig in the mud?   no ○ yes ●
4. Did the pup tug on rugs?   no ○ yes ●

Write a title for the story. **Answers will vary.**

Tell a friend what might happen next in the story.

Language arts application; reading and answering comprehension questions with short u words.

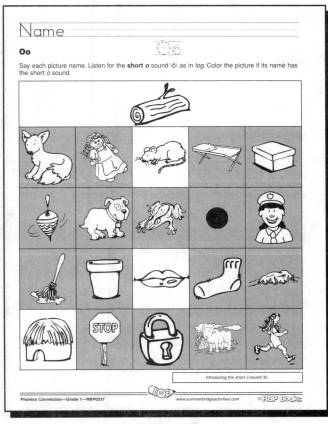

Page 68

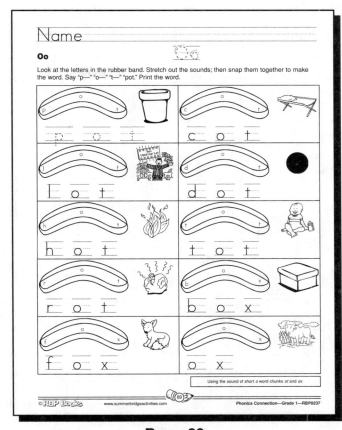

Page 69

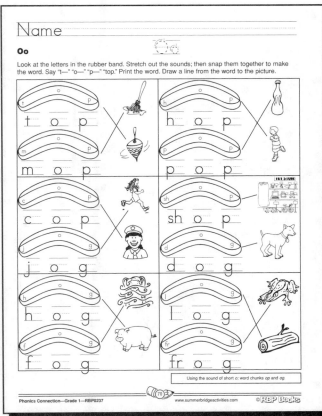

Page 70

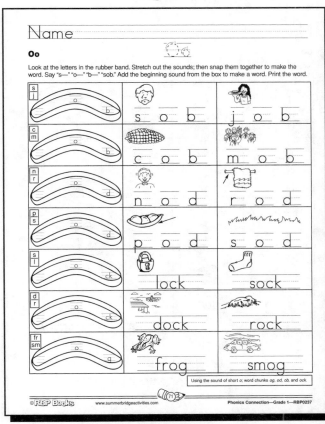

Page 71

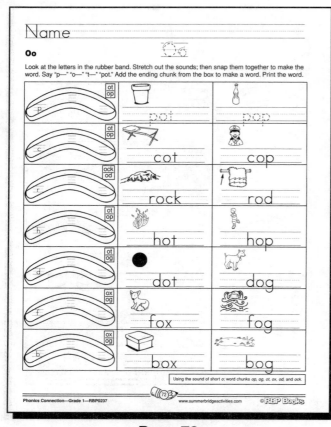

Page 72

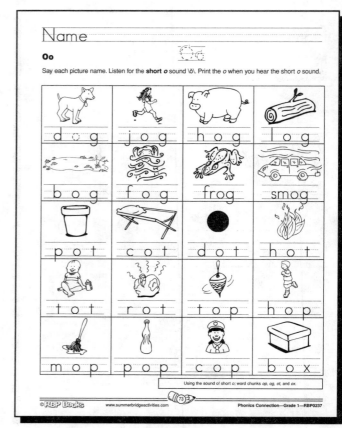

Page 73

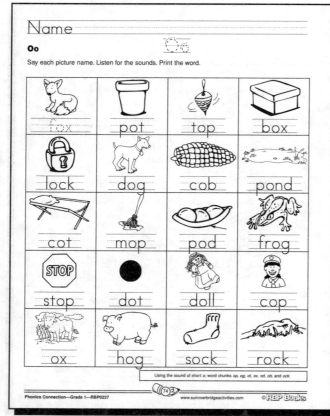

Page 74

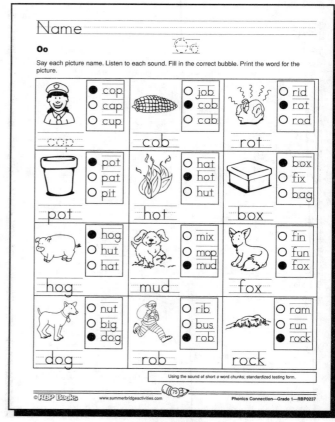

Page 75

Answer Pages

Page 78

Name

Oo

Read each sentence. Print a word that rhymes with the underlined word. Make the sentence tell about the picture to the right.

1. The fox is in the box
2. A hog sat in a pond
3. I will not jog in the fog
4. The pot is hot
5. The frog is on the log
6. The cot has a spot (or dot).
7. Ron and the cop can hop
8. Rod had to stop at the shop

Using language arts; using context clues to select rhyming words with short o word chunks.

Phonics Connection—Grade 1—RBP0237 · www.summerbridgeactivities.com · ©RBP Books

Page 78

Page 79

Name

Oo

Read each sentence. Read the three words. Look at the picture. Fill in the bubble next to the word that makes sense in the sentence. Print the word on the line.

1. Dot can hop like a frog ● frog ○ log ○ bat
2. Ron put the doll in a box ● box ○ bib ○ hat
3. John got the mop for his mom. ● mop ○ bus ○ bag
4. The tot can draw dots. ● dots ○ hogs ○ tops
5. The fox hid in the log. ○ mud ○ sub ● log
6. Todd can do a good job. ● job ○ jog ○ song

Using language arts; using context clues to select missing words with short o word chunks.

©RBP Books · www.summerbridgeactivities.com · Phonics Connection—Grade 1—RBP0237

Page 79

Page 80

Name

Oo

Read the words. Look at the picture. Write the words in the correct order to match the picture.

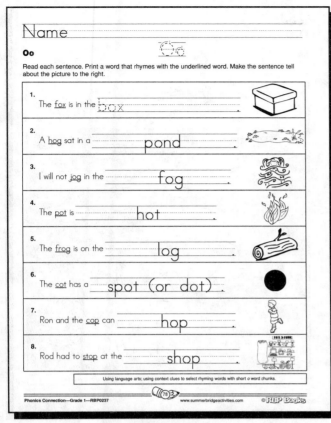

The	the
fox	on
is	box

The box is on the fox.

cop	the
is	on
The	pop

The pop is on the cop.

dog	the
fog	in
The	is

The dog is in the fog.

the	tot
cot	on
is	The

The tot is on the cot.

Using language arts; using context clues to write sentences; word chunks op, og, ot, and ox.

Phonics Connection—Grade 1—RBP0237 · www.summerbridgeactivities.com · ©RBP Books

Page 80

Page 81

Name

Oo

Write the name of the picture. Read the sentences below and color each picture. Underline the **short o** words in each sentence.

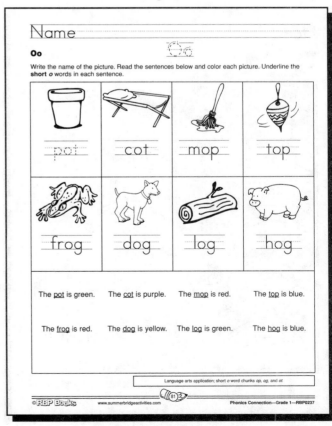

pot   cot   mop   top

frog   dog   log   hog

The pot is green. The cot is purple. The mop is red. The top is blue.

The frog is red. The dog is yellow. The log is green. The hog is blue.

Language arts application; short o word chunks op, og, and ot.

©RBP Books · www.summerbridgeactivities.com · Phonics Connection—Grade 1—RBP0237

Page 81

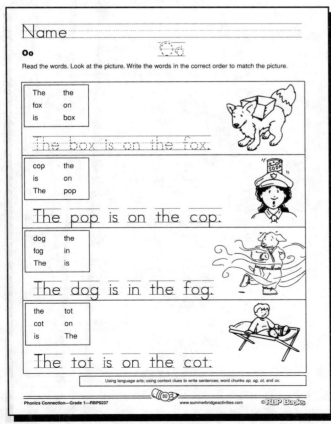

Phonics Connection—Grade 1—RBP0237

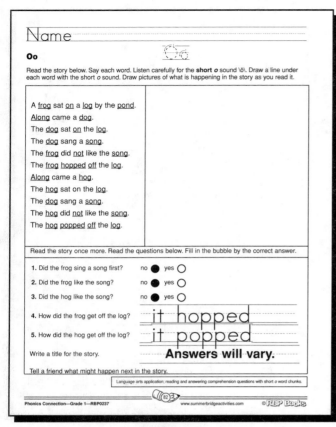

Page 82

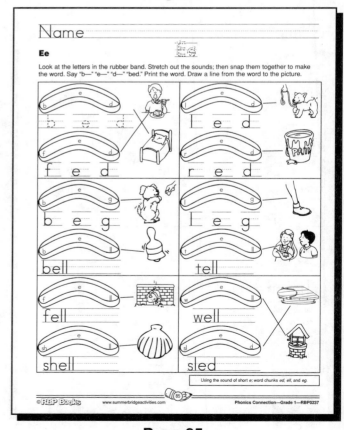

Page 83

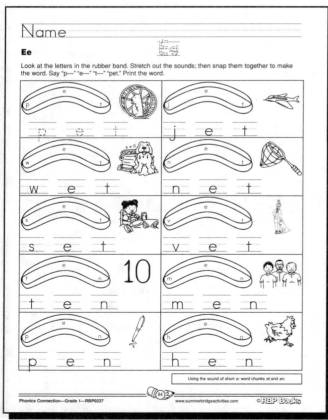

Page 84

Page 85

Answer Pages

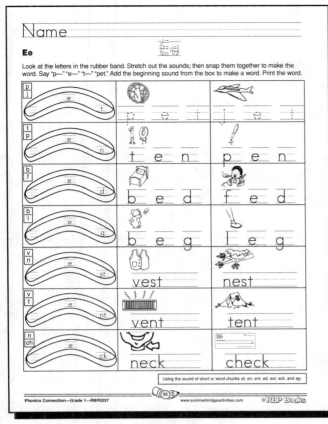

Page 86

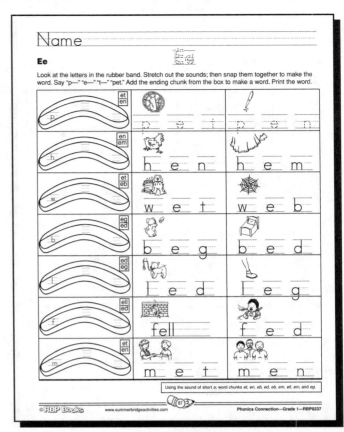

Page 87

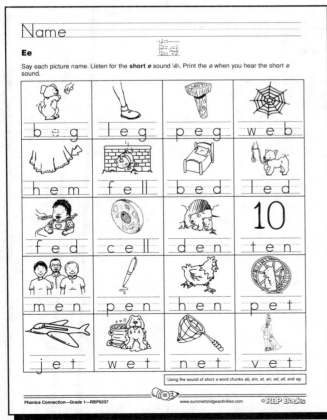

Page 88

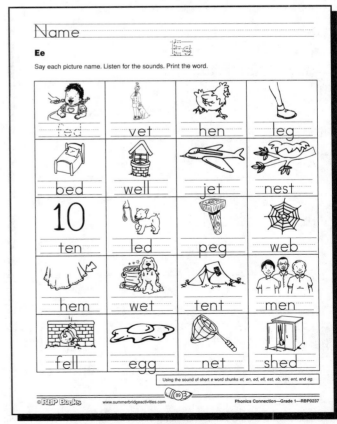

Page 89

Page 90

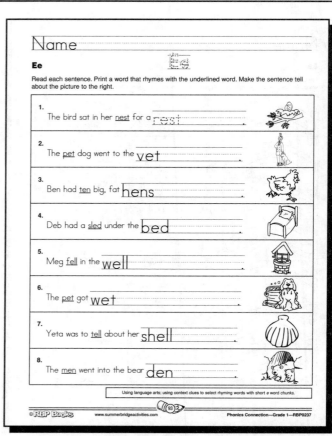

Page 93

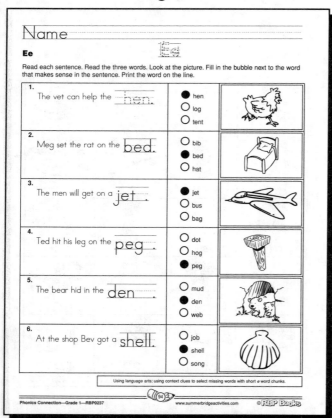

Page 94

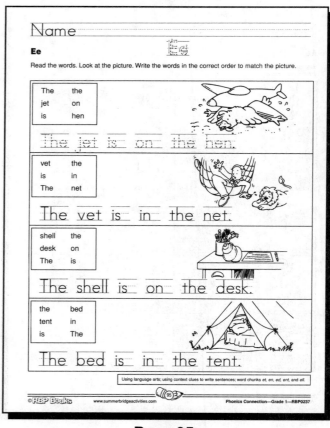

Page 95

Answer Pages

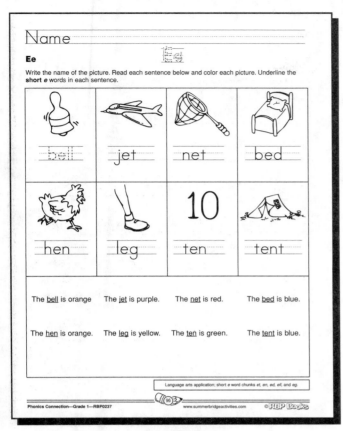

Page 96

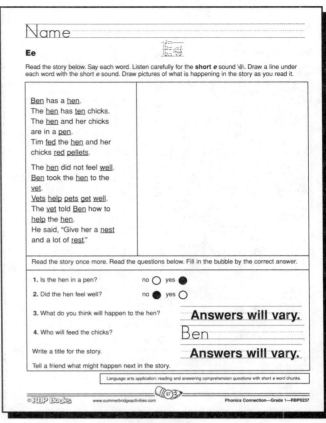

Page 97

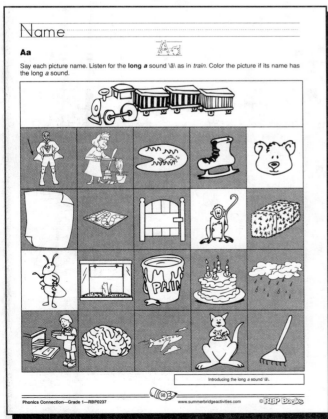

Page 98

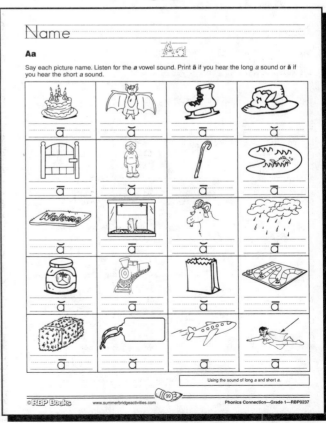

Page 99

Answer Pages

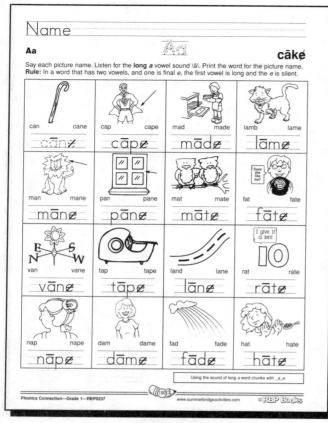

Page 100

Page 101

Page 102

Page 103

Answer Pages

Page 104

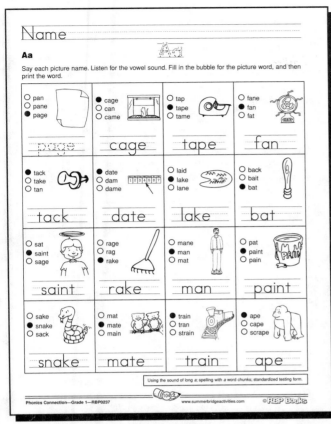

Name

Aa

Say each picture name. Listen for the vowel sound. Fill in the bubble for the picture word, and then print the word.

- ○ pan
- ○ pane
- ● page

page

- ● cage
- ○ can
- ○ came

cage

- ○ tap
- ● tape
- ○ tame

tape

- ● fane
- ● fan
- ○ fat

fan

- ● tack
- ○ take
- ○ tan

tack

- ● date
- ○ dam
- ○ dame

date

- ○ laid
- ● lake
- ○ lane

lake

- ○ back
- ○ bait
- ● bat

bat

- ○ sat
- ● saint
- ○ sage

saint

- ○ rage
- ○ rag
- ● rake

rake

- ○ mane
- ● man
- ○ mat

man

- ○ pat
- ● paint
- ○ pain

paint

- ○ sake
- ● snake
- ○ sack

snake

- ○ mat
- ● mate
- ○ main

mate

- ● train
- ○ tran
- ○ strain

train

- ● ape
- ○ cape
- ○ scrape

ape

Using the sound of long a; spelling with a word chunks; standardized testing form.

Phonics Connection—Grade 1—RBP0237 www.summerbridgeactivities.com © RBP Books

Page 105

Name

Aa

Read each sentence. Read the three words. Look at the picture. Fill in the bubble next to the word that makes sense in the sentence. Print the word on the line.

1. Dan **ate** the cake.
   - ● ate
   - ○ at
   - ○ gate

2. Is the bat in the **cave** ?
   - ○ case
   - ● cave
   - ○ can

3. Dad put the **mat** into the box.
   - ● mat
   - ○ maid
   - ○ may

4. Sue will **play** the game.
   - ● play
   - ○ page
   - ○ make

5. Jim will **rake** the grass.
   - ● rake
   - ○ rat
   - ○ rage

6. At the shop Bev got a **cage**.
   - ○ came
   - ● cage
   - ○ cave

Using language arts; using context clues to select missing words with a sound.

© RBP Books www.summerbridgeactivities.com Phonics Connection—Grade 1—RBP0237

Page 106

Name

Aa

Read the story below. Say each word. Listen carefully for the **long a** sound \ā\. Draw a line under each word with the long a sound. Draw pictures of what is happening in the story as you read it.

May lived in Spain.
One day it began to rain.
May baked a cake.
The cake looked like a snail.

She sailed on the lake.
She gave the cake to a friend.
Her friend's name was Cane.

Cane lived in a cave.
He was very brave.
Cane and May ate the snail cake.

Read the story once more. Read the questions below. Fill in the bubble by the correct answer.

1. Was it a rainy day?   no ○   yes ●
2. Did May make a cage?   no ●   yes ○
3. Did May sail to a cave?   no ●   yes ○
4. How do you think Cane felt when May gave him the cake? **Answers will vary.**

Write a title for the story. **Answers will vary.**
Tell a friend what might happen next in the story.

Language arts application; reading and answering comprehension questions with long a word chunks.

Phonics Connection—Grade 1—RBP0237 www.summerbridgeactivities.com © RBP Books

Page 107

Name

Ii

Say each picture name. Listen for the **long i** sound \ī\ as in slide. Color the picture if its name has the long i sound.

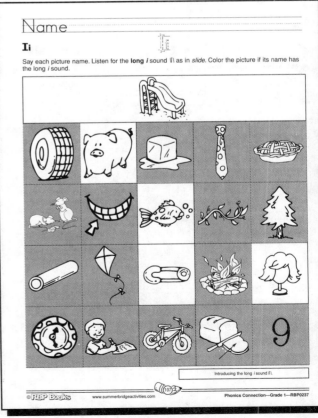

Introducing the long i sound \ī\.

© RBP Books www.summerbridgeactivities.com Phonics Connection—Grade 1—RBP0237

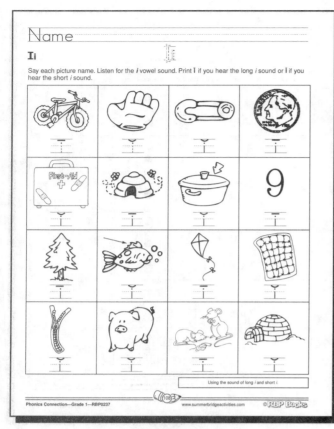

Page 108

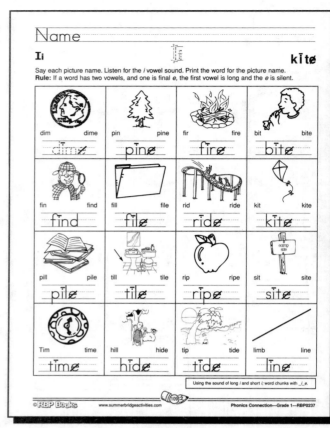

Page 109

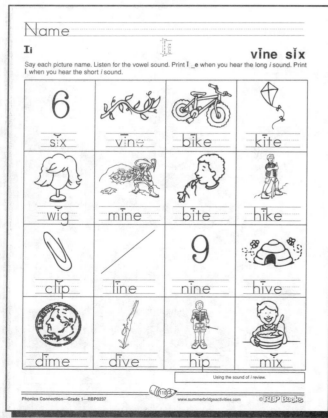

Page 110

Page 111

Page 112

Name

I i

Read each sentence. Read the three words. Look at the picture. Fill in the bubble next to the word that makes sense in the sentence. Print the word on the line.

1. The ~~kite~~ can fly high.
   ● kite
   ○ kit
   ○ Kate

2. I can **dive**.
   ● dive
   ○ dim
   ○ date

3. Kate likes to **hide**.
   ● hide
   ○ hate
   ○ hat

4. Teddy had two **mice** for pets.
   ○ met
   ○ make
   ● mice

5. We had a piece of **pie**.
   ● pie
   ○ pet
   ○ pat

6. The bees flew in their **hive**.
   ● hive
   ○ high
   ○ have

Using language arts; using context clues to select missing words with long *i* word chunks.

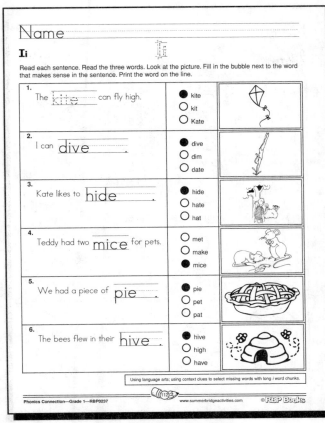

Phonics Connection—Grade 1—RBP0237   www.summerbridgeactivities.com   ©RBP Books

Page 113

Name

I i

Read the story below. Say each word. Listen carefully for the **long** *i* sound /ī/. Draw a line under each word with the long *i* sound. Draw pictures of what is happening in the story as you read it.

Mike likes to ride his bike.
Six mice like to hide on the
bike with Mike.
Mike can bike for a mile.
He likes to go up to the top of
the hills.
He can go high into the pines.

Mike's bike gets a flat tire.
He has to take time to fix it.
It starts to rain.
The mice help him fix the tire.

Read the story once more. Read the questions below. Fill in the bubble by the correct answer.

1. Do five mice like to go with Mike?   no ●   yes ○
2. Does Mike like to bike?   no ○   yes ●
3. Will Mike ride high into the pines?   no ○   yes ●
4. Who likes to ride the bike besides Mike?   **six mice**

Write a title for the story.   **Answers will vary.**

Tell a friend what might happen next in the story.

Language arts application; reading and answering comprehension questions with long *i* word chunks.

©RBP Books   www.summerbridgeactivities.com   Phonics Connection—Grade 1—RBP0237

Page 114

Name

U u

Say each picture name. Listen for the **long** *u* sound /ū/ as in *ruler*. Color the picture if its name has the long *u* sound.

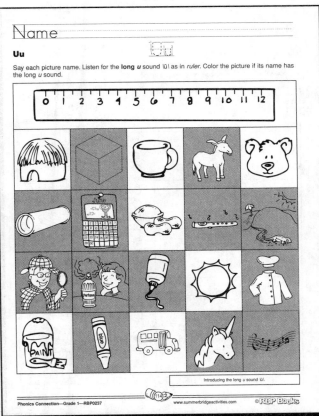

Introducing the long *u* sound /ū/.

Phonics Connection—Grade 1—RBP0237   www.summerbridgeactivities.com   ©RBP Books

Page 115

Name

U u

Say each picture name. Listen for the *u* vowel sound. Print ū if you hear the long *u* sound or ŭ if you hear the short *u* sound.

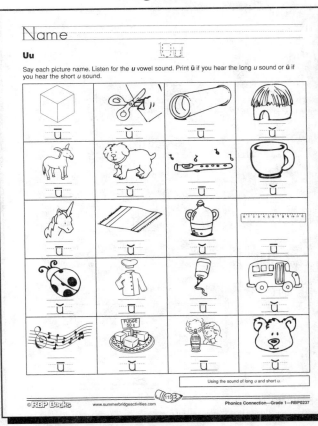

Using the sound of long *u* and short *u*.

©RBP Books   www.summerbridgeactivities.com   Phonics Connection—Grade 1—RBP0237

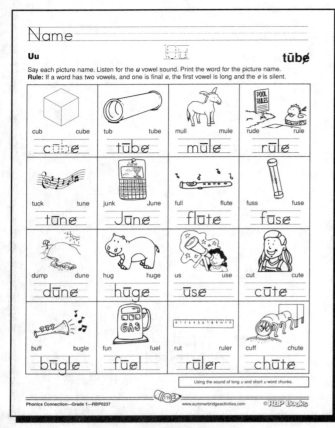

Page 116

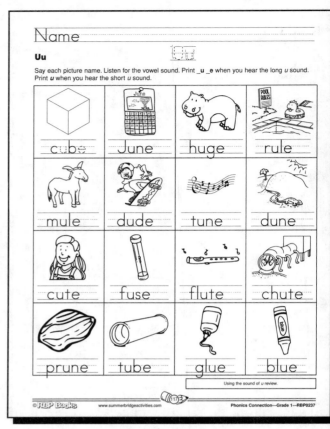

Page 117

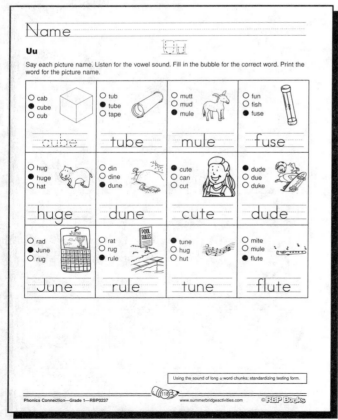

Page 118

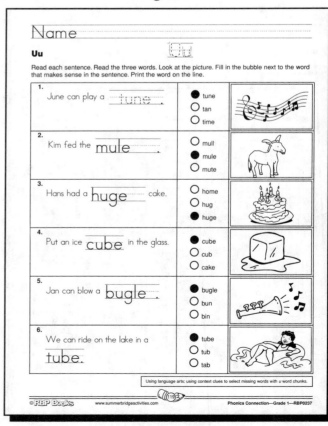

Page 119

Answer Pages

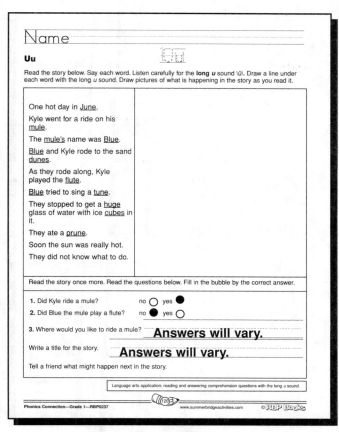

Page 120

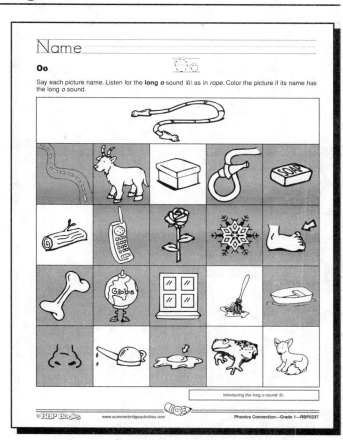

Page 121

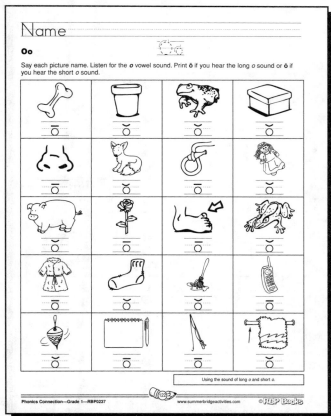

Page 122

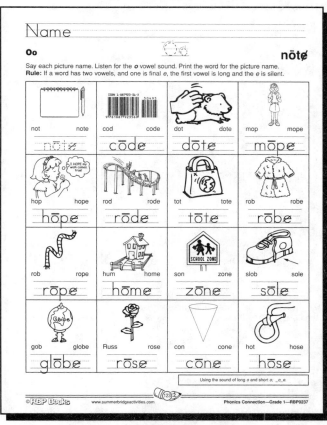

Page 123

www.summerbridgeactivities.com
Phonics Connection—Grade 1—RBP0237

Answer Pages

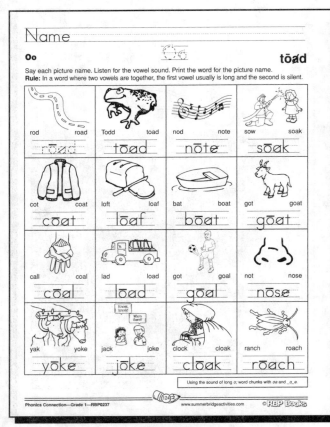

Page 124

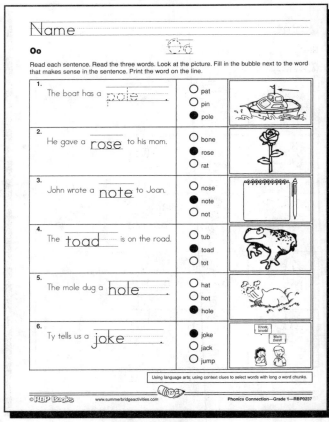

Page 125

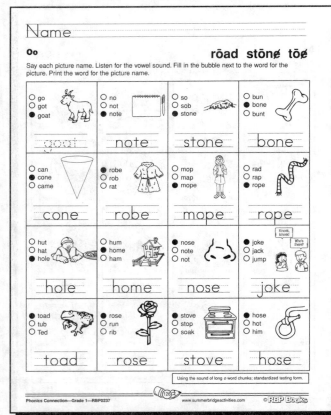

Page 126

Page 127

Name

Oo

Read each sentence. Read the three words. Look at the picture. Fill in the bubble next to the word that makes sense in the sentence. Print the word on the line.

1. The boat has a __pole__.
   ○ pat ○ pin ● pole

2. He gave a __rose__ to his mom.
   ○ bone ● rose ○ rat

3. John wrote a __note__ to Joan.
   ○ nose ● note ○ not

4. The __toad__ is on the road.
   ○ tub ● toad ○ tot

5. The mole dug a __hole__.
   ○ hat ○ hot ● hole

6. Ty tells us a __joke__.
   ● joke ○ jack ○ jump

Using language arts; using context clues to select words with long o word chunks.

Page 127

186

Answer Pages

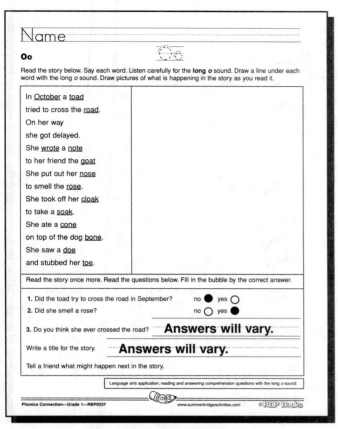

Page 128

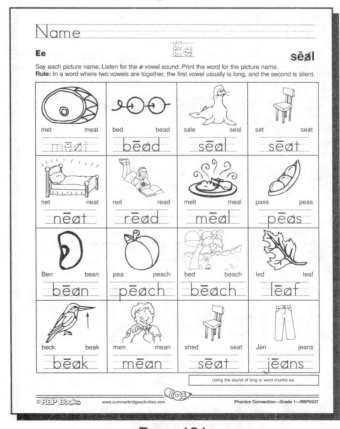

Page 129

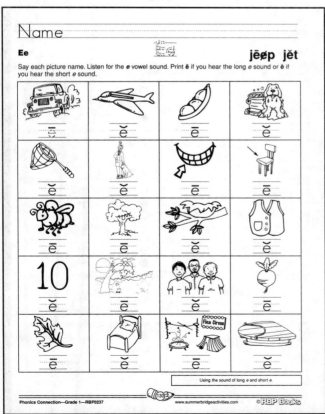

Page 130

Page 131

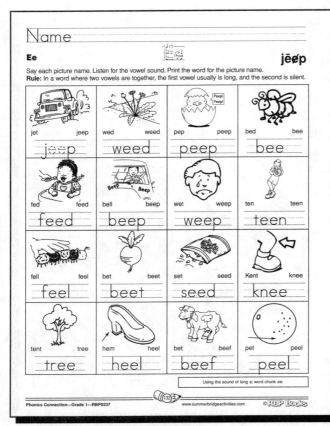

Page 132

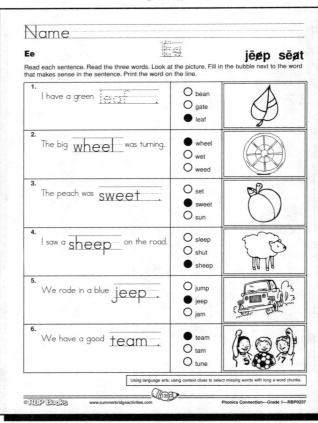

Page 133

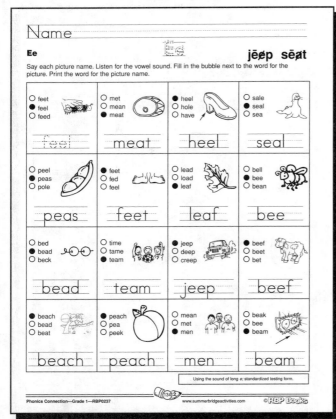

Page 134

Read each sentence. Read the three words. Look at the picture. Fill in the bubble next to the word that makes sense in the sentence. Print the word on the line.

1. I have a green _leaf_	○ bean ○ gate ● leaf	
2. The big _wheel_ was turning.	● wheel ○ wet ○ weed	
3. The peach was _sweet_.	○ set ● sweet ○ sun	
4. I saw a _sheep_ on the road.	○ sleep ○ shut ● sheep	
5. We rode in a blue _jeep_.	○ jump ● jeep ○ jam	
6. We have a good _team_.	● team ○ tam ○ tune	

Using language arts; using context clues to select missing words with long e word chunks.

Page 135

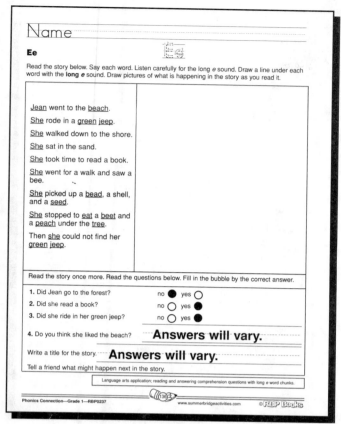

Page 136

Page 137

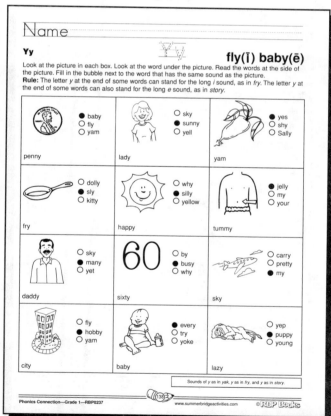

Page 138

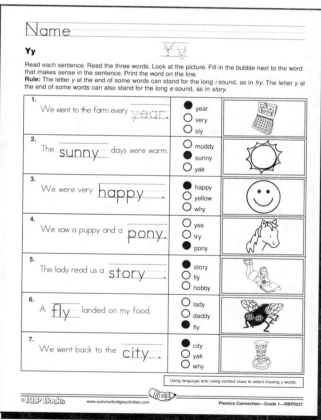

Page 139

Page 140

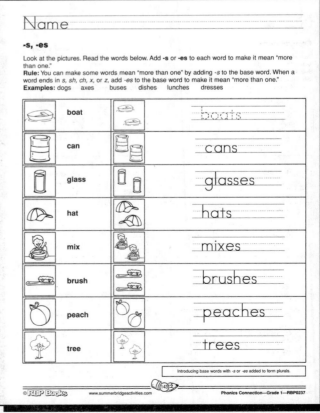

Page 141

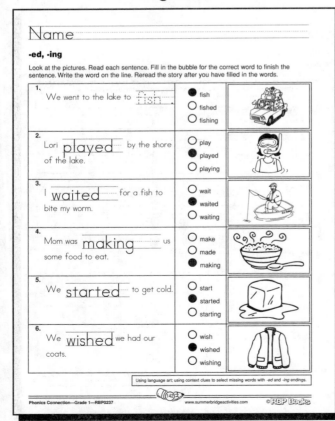

Page 142

Page 143

Answer Pages

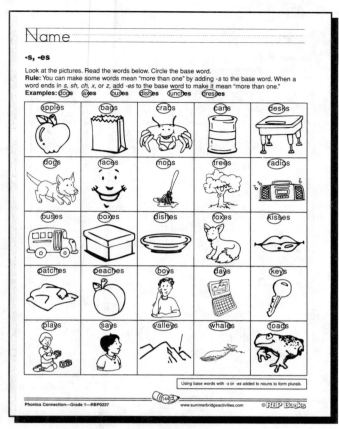

Page 144

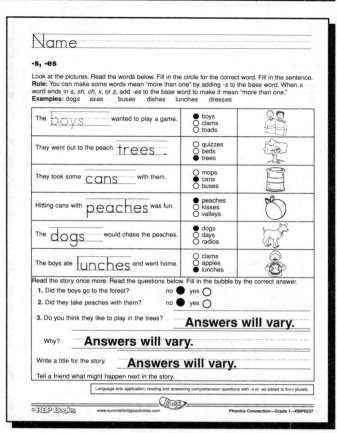

Page 145

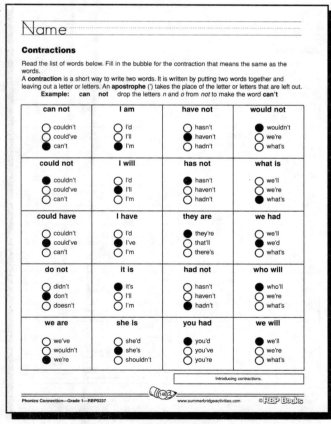

Page 146

Name

Contractions

Read each contraction below. Then write the two words for which each contraction stands.

A **contraction** is a short way to write two words. It is written by putting two words together and leaving out a letter or letters. An **apostrophe** (') takes the place of the letter or letters that are left out.

    Example: you   are   drop the letter *a* from *are* to make the word **you're**

you're	you	are
she'd	she	had, would
they've	they	have
that's	that	is
didn't	did	not
let's	let	us
he'll	he	will
isn't	is	not

Using contractions.

Page 147

Answer Pages

Page 148

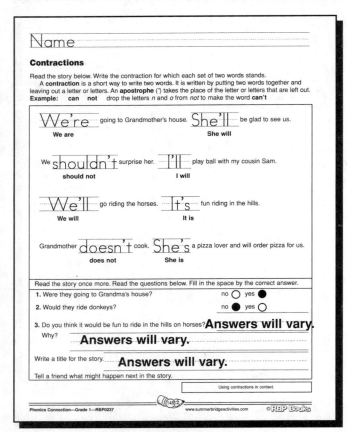

Name

Contractions

Read the story below. Write the contraction for which each set of two words stands.
A **contraction** is a short way to write two words. It is written by putting two words together and leaving out a letter or letters. An **apostrophe** (') takes the place of the letter or letters that are left out.
Example: can not — drop the letters *n* and *o* from *not* to make the word **can't**

We're going to Grandmother's house. She'll be glad to see us.
We are — **She will**

We shouldn't surprise her. I'll play ball with my cousin Sam.
should not — **I will**

We'll go riding the horses. It's fun riding in the hills.
We will — **It is**

Grandmother doesn't cook. She's a pizza lover and will order pizza for us.
does not — **She is**

Read the story once more. Read the questions below. Fill in the space by the correct answer.
1. Were they going to Grandma's house?   no ○   yes ●
2. Would they ride donkeys?   no ●   yes ○
3. Do you think it would be fun to ride in the hills on horses? **Answers will vary.**
Why? **Answers will vary.**

Write a title for the story. **Answers will vary.**

Tell a friend what might happen next in the story.

Using contractions in context.

Phonics Connection—Grade 1—RBP0237   www.summerbridgeactivities.com   © RBP Books

Page 148

Page 149

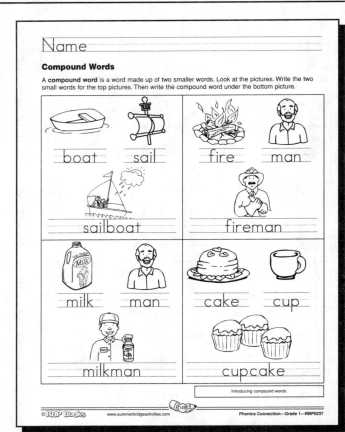

Name

Compound Words

A **compound word** is a word made up of two smaller words. Look at the pictures. Write the two small words for the top pictures. Then write the compound word under the bottom picture.

boat   sail
sailboat

fire   man
fireman

milk   man
milkman

cake   cup
cupcake

Introducing compound words.

© RBP Books   www.summerbridgeactivities.com   Phonics Connection—Grade 1—RBP0237

Page 149

Page 150

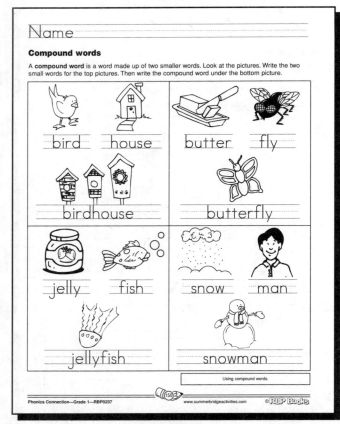

Name

Compound words

A **compound word** is a word made up of two smaller words. Look at the pictures. Write the two small words for the top pictures. Then write the compound word under the bottom picture.

bird   house
birdhouse

butter   fly
butterfly

jelly   fish
jellyfish

snow   man
snowman

Using compound words.

Phonics Connection—Grade 1—RBP0237   www.summerbridgeactivities.com   © RBP Books

Page 150

Page 152

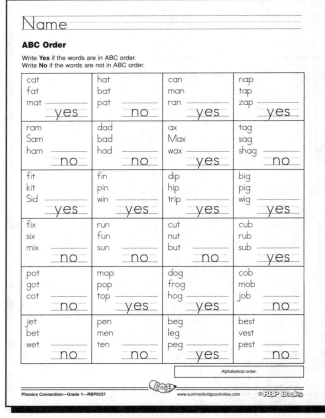

Name

ABC Order

Write **Yes** if the words are in ABC order.
Write **No** if the words are not in ABC order.

cat fat mat ___ **yes**	hat bat pat ___ **no**	can man ran ___ **yes**	nap tap zap ___ **yes**
ram Sam ham ___ **no**	dad bad had ___ **no**	ax Max wax ___ **yes**	tag sag shag ___ **no**
fit kit Sid ___ **yes**	fin pin win ___ **yes**	dip hip trip ___ **yes**	big pig wig ___ **yes**
fix six mix ___ **no**	run fun sun ___ **no**	cut nut but ___ **no**	cub rub sub ___ **yes**
pot got cot ___ **no**	mop pop top ___ **yes**	dog frog hog ___ **yes**	cob mob job ___ **no**
jet bet wet ___ **no**	pen men ten ___ **no**	beg leg peg ___ **yes**	best vest pest ___ **no**

Alphabetical order.

Phonics Connection—Grade 1—RBP0237   www.summerbridgeactivities.com   © RBP Books

Page 152